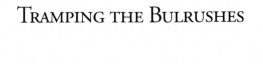

TRAMPING THE BULRUSHES

that the analogy is itself inherent, that meaning is itself analogy, that there wld be nothing if it were not itself an image

—Charles Olson to Jeremy Prynne, 11 January 1964

TRAMPING THE BULRUSHES

John Clarke

Edited and with a preface by Michael Boughn
Introduction by Lisa Jarnot
Afterword by Daniel Zimmerman

Dispatches Editions

"Lots of Doom" was first published by Cotinneh Books, Castlegar, B.C., in 1975. It was republished by *shuffaloff*/Eternal Network in 2012.

"The Metaphysics of Survival" was first presented to the "Radical Poetries/Critical Address" Conference at SUNY Buffalo in April, 1988. It was first printed in *Acts* 10, 1 April 1989.

"Olson: the Book," first appeared in **intent.** 2.4-3.1 (Winter/Spring 1991).

"Tramping the Bulrushes" first appeared as "Disch's Dis" in **intent.** 3.2-3 (Summer/Fall 1991). It was reprinted as a chapbook, "Tramping the Bulrushes," by *shuffaloff* in 2005.

Thanks to the Poetry/Rare Book Collection at the University at Buffalo for their assistance with the archival materials.

Front cover photo: John Clarke and Harvey Brown in Gloucester Harbor, 198?, by Rose Belforti.
Back cover photo: John Clarke and Charles Olson at Onetto's, 1965, by Fred Wah.
Photo p. 8 by Michael Boughn
Photo p. 78 by June Ava Posner
Photo p. 122 by B. Cass Clarke
Photo p. 158 by Fred Wah
Photo p. 171 by B.Cass Clarke.
Photo p. 186 by Michael Boughn
Photo p. 270 by Paula Satow.
Photo p. 287 by Bradley Deans

Library of Congress Cataloging-In-Publication Data applied for.

ISBN 978-1-944682-86-6

Dispatches Editions is an imprint of Spuyten Duyvil Press

Contents

PREFACE

JOHN (JACK) CLARKE AND CHARLES OLSON first met in the spring
of 1964 at Albert Cook's house in Buffalo, New York. The previous
year Cook had recruited Olson to teach at the newly expanded
State University of New York at Buffalo, offering him free reign
with courses in both modern poetry and myth. Cook, who had directed
Clarke's dissertation on William Blake, was also trying to hire him away
from the University of Illinois, Champagne-Urbana and invited him
to Buffalo for a job interview. Clarke came to the interview knowing
nothing of Olson, and with several reservations about the possible move
to Buffalo. After the job interview, there was a party at Cook's house.
Clarke recalls:

> Later that night Charles came down to the party. I was sitting on
> a straight chair by the fireplace and he sat down on the couch,
> like so ⎯ • and the connection was instaneous—maybe that's
> a new word, I meant instantaneous, but like that one better, it
> accents the sta etymon . . .. Olson's report of the meeting, as
> someone later told me, was that he dug my pants, the material
> they were made of, and the way I was sitting with my legs
> crossed. Upshot of course was that all other considerations were
> blown away: I was coming to Buffalo.[1]

It was a turning point in both men's lives. The relationship was mutually
generative and productive. Olson, among other things, got Blake, a
visionary poet who became increasingly important in his thinking, from
Clarke. He also got the loyal friendship of a remarkable person with a
brilliant, unorthodox mind who was interested in and able to keep up
with his cosmological venturing.

It was the first time Olson had taught since Black Mountain College. He dove into his topics with fervour, exploring and developing his own thinking along with his students', pushing into realms of deep cosmological space following his understanding that poetry is a mode of knowing, what he called "animate" ("the aboriginal instance of activity") and essential: "I am here seeking to speak within, or across the 'range' of a principle of likeness which includes, and seeks to 'cover' what Henry Corbin reminds me is a constantly affirmed homology among the initiatic cosmos, the world of nature, and the celestial world."[2]

As early as 1962 at Goddard College, Olson had expressed his rejection of the literary and, implicitly, the professionalization of American poetry, including the drift of the New American poets into that range of political compromise.[3] As Fred Wah put it, Olson

> was 'ideologically' insisting on a certain "attention" to the politics of poetry and his particular map of Amurican poetry. Eg: In September 1964, as I think I've mentioned to you, in our first class, he erased Drummond Hadley from the map, the only poet remaining from the previous year. This had to do with Drum's decision to not publish his book with Harvey [Brown's Frontier Press]. That is, O still had definite ideas about poetry as a social and political possibility. Both the Goddard (I would guess) and the Berkeley were him performing the necessary resistance to the poetry world's appropriation of the NAP.[4]

This move was entangled with his reading and teaching at Buffalo and the dimensions into which his thinking was tropologically leading ("of tip and end / of gravity"), setting the stage for the scandalous Event he enacted at the 1965 Berkeley Poetry Conference that left so many of his former friends dumbfounded and even hostile.

From 1963 through the death of Betty Kaiser, his wife, in a car crash in March, 1964, to the Berkeley Conference, until he finally turned his myth class over to Clarke and left Buffalo for good in September, 1965, Olson's thinking and writing were intricately tied to his work with his students in Buffalo and his rejection of a poetry world that was increasingly professionalized. Clarke was close to Olson through all of that. *The Magazine of Further Studies,* which was published by the students in Olson's courses, including Clarke, stands as a still living example of the rejection of the institutionalized literary.

For his part, Clarke found his intellectual and artistic life redefined in terms of a company of scholars and poets crystallizing around Olson's prodigious and provocative cosmogonic energies. He became a self-described student of Olson's, or as he puts it in one of the essays included here, a novice, as in Novalis's *Novices of Saïs*. He had a popular poster framed on his dining room wall, an image of a boy seated next to an elephant, his small arm heroically and lovingly embracing what he can reach of the massive figure next to him. That, Jack said, was an image of his relation to Charles. It was not a relation that many men (or women), especially literary heroes, could entertain. But Jack was about as far from those inherently individualistic modes of being—and the thought of rewards—as it is possible to imagine; not anti, just somewhere else entirely, patiently doing, as Emerson proposed, his work: "My life is not for spectacle. But do your work and I will know you."

While that work went on in relation to Olson, it is not accurate to speak of it in terms of "Olson's influence" on Clarke because the dynamic of their relationship differed fundamentally from the relation such a phrase implies. They travelled in the company of each other's thinking. Clarke found a boundless potential there, a thinking that resonated with Blake's thinking, opening into otherwise occulted complexities of our strange condition.

Clarke was always further. His reading of Blake, which went on constantly, took him into depths of gnosis that made him the primary transmission point for Blake's thinking in the twentieth century. No one else absorbed Blake to the degree that Clarke did, turning that thought/poetry/vision into a poetics of the.full intensity, an emergent thinking. As an accomplished jazz pianist—he toured with a band in his youth—he brought a practicing jazz musician's ear to the poetic line. His understanding of improvisation was thoroughly grounded in a musical knowledge of rhythm and measure, so that his thinking/knowing is inextricable from musical being.

And by thinking, I mean poetry. After meeting Olson, poetry became the centre of every dimension of Jack's life. By and large, as the thousands of unpublished poems in his notebooks testify to, most of his mental work went into the thinking of poetry, or poetry's thinking, or *thinkingpoetry,* which he understood, like Olson, to be a specific and untranslatable mode of knowing. The piece which opens this selection, "Lots of Doom," is his homage to Olson's Berkeley "reading" and embodies that chiasmic identity, moving back and forth, in and out of thinking/talking/poetry as if they were interchangeable. Albert Glover's editing of Clarke's writing in "toward a #6" reveals the same mutil-valenced mind at work/play in language, including letters, poems, and reading/bibliography, all facets of the same lively attention. So does the dance of mind among the varied selections that compose this book, the lively thinking that charges every word with vision and energy.

Clarke moved, as Al Cook stated, as far beyond Olson as Olson moved beyond Pound. For Clarke, the destiny of poetry was what Blake called four-fold vision, a state of being in which the plentitude of the world is fully engaged in creative entangled *workplay,* the full realization of the creative. In *From Feathers to Iron*, his masterwork on poetics, he calls it "the strengthening method of world completion," a task particularly urgent given the world historical crisis, the broken Sampo, we find ourselves in. Myth is a crucial part of that undertaking because myth's figures and stories are modes (forms) of knowing the world's timeless energies, energies that shape and fuel our lives. But so was science, itself a kind myth yeilding a particular knowing of the world's being. And the unfolding dramas of contemporary politics. These were all dimensions of the depth of the world he pointed out, its information. The poetry included here enacts that thinking as it traverses the difficult, shattered condition of the post-modern world.

Beginning shortly after Olson's death, the 1970's saw a growing criticism of Olson's reputation and his work from several directions. Perhaps the reaction was inevitable, given the enormous authority that people had invested in him, even if he had not asked for it. But the professionalism that Olson abjured took hold with a vengeance as the culture of rapture, rupture, and transgression gave way to the era of Reagan and Thatcher, and the conservatism that filtered through the common world, even when it proposed itself as "avant-garde." It was not kind to Olson.

The metamorphosis of Olson's reputation was not unlike the cycle of Blake's "Mental Traveller," the poem Frances Boldereff sent to Olson in 1950, with its vision of the inevitable cycles of revolution and reaction, creative release and containment. As Blake has it in his poem, the energy and imagination that Olson represents are nailed to a rock and bound with iron thorns. By the early 90's Olson's character and contribution were subjected to serious, often negative, revision.[5] Clarke argued quietly but resolutely against that sad fact, even as he recognized the overwhelming forces lining up against him, including importantly some of Olson's former friends who couldn't accept the continuing transformations which took him beyond the literary world that they were committed to.

The three essays on Olson were Clarke's final, reasoned gestures of resistance to the portrait of a monstrous Olson typified by Thomas Disch's glowing review of Tom Clark's biography, *Charles Olson, the Allegory of a Poet's Life*,[6] and to concurrent attempts to reduce Olson to simply a poet of "historical geography." They were also his assertion of the lasting value of Olson's unmatched contribution to the thinking of our condition at the bloody end of modern oblivion and, once again, the Babe . . .. The love and respect they embody resonate with a quiet brilliance and insight that will endure.

– Michael Boughn, Toronto, 24 January 2017

Notes:

[1] John Clarke to Tom Clark, October 23, 1986

[2] "The Animate vs. the Mechanical, and Thought." In *Collected Prose*. Ed. Donald Allen and Benjamin Friedlander. Berkeley: University of California Press, 1997.

[3] See *Charles Olson at Goddard College*, April 12-14, 1962. Ed. Kyle Schlesinger. Houston: Cuneiform Press, 2011.

[4] Personal email correspondence dated 31 August 2016.

[5] See my essay, "Poetics Bodies: Charles Olson and Some Poetry Wars, 1913-1990." At *Dispatches from the Poetry Wars* (http://dispatchespoetry.com/articles/commentary/2016/04/55) April 2016.

[6] Thomas Disch's review of Clark's book first appeared as "Iambic Megalomania" in the *Los Angeles Times*, April 18, 1991. It was reprinted as "The High Priest of High Times" in *The Castle of Indolence*, NY: Picador USA, 1996

CLARKE'S CURRICULUM:
UNDER THE DOME OF HOMER

Lisa Jarnot

"Sometimes paranoia's just having all the facts."
—William Burroughs

"shall you uncover honey / where maggots are?"
—Charles Olson

I DON'T REMEMBER ANYONE TELLING ME I should study with Jack Clarke. I was vaguely an English major at the University of Buffalo, but I avoided classes when I could: I fancied myself a political activist (Green Party) and poet (Beatnik). It was my junior year—I was nineteen—when I signed up for "Approaches to Literature: Mythology (Greek and Roman)", taught by "Clarke". Needless to say I was suspicious of professors and academia as a whole. I'd attached myself to Bob Creeley the previous year and had no regrets about that. Creeley may have been in the English Department, but he didn't walk the walk. Anyone who bummed cigarettes off the students and queried "You dig?" to a roomful of Long Island sorority girls had my full respect. Jack was a little bit harder to read. He could pass for a professor, ambling down the halls of the English Department wearing his tweed suit jacket and carrying a briefcase. But something amazing transpired in the classroom. On day one he peered at us over his big glasses, chewed on his lip a little bit, his bushy eyebrows undulating like caterpillars, and then he said it: "Mythology is about what happened before the System

took over." I stopped doodling and looked up from my notebook as
he continued: "Mythology is needed in places where lots of things are
happening in order to arrange and understand reality." I imagine in
retrospect that Jack surveyed the room to see if he could separate the
sheep from the goats— he was looking for operatives. Professors didn't
talk about "the System" in a tone of voice that conjured Abbie Hoffman
or Lenny Bruce. Here, in a depressingly plastic classroom, tweedy Dr.
Clarke with his briefcase at his side, was going to turn us onto The
Metamorphoses of Ovid, The Homeric Hymns, the Iliad, the Odyssey,
and the stories of how we had gotten into the mess that we were in
because of this thing called the System.

I didn't know at the time that Charles Olson's influence was lurking in
Jack's thinking. Olson came up in passing in those first weeks of class
when Jack mentioned him as a guide to "how a poet works with mytho-
logical material." I had just begun to excavate Olson—partly through a
graduate seminar of Bob Creeley's, and partly through Robert Duncan's
essays. Olson was still too big for me—I could revel in the particulars
of his moonsets and tansy buttons, but the scale of the work geographi-
cally, historically, and philosophically, was well beyond me. (In 1995
when I finally made a pilgrimage to Gloucester the poems all fell into
place and Maximus was finally mine.)

In the classroom and in private conversations, Jack always had a light
touch when it came to Olson. It's something I appreciate now— the
fact that he intrinsically trusted me to find my way to the poets I
needed when I needed them. He seemed to draw almost equally out
of a constellation of minds: Olson and Duncan and Blake definitely,
and also Joanne Kyger, Anselm Hollo, and Ed Sanders. Later, when
I came to realize that there was all-out warfare in poetry circles (was
the "Projective" an exercise in cock-waving? Were all our stories lost as
Language poets experimented away from the mytho-poetic?) I was glad
that I could refer to Jack as my mentor. He'd never asked me to become
an acolyte in an Olsonian lineage, and he planted a seed for me to later
love Olson's poetry. When I disagreed with Jack (I remember stomping
out of his office on more than one occasion because we didn't see eye to
eye on some issue or another) he seemed to welcome my strides toward
independent thinking.

Reading now his responses to Tom Clark's 1991 biography of Olson, it
strikes me that Jack must have felt besieged and lonely (he was dying of

cancer, the English Department was undergoing a transformation away from the era of Olson, and the Los Angeles Times somehow felt it useful to publish a piece by Tom Disch that was not so much a review of Tom Clark's biography as an all-out character-assassination of Olson). What I see in Jack's response is what I saw in him as a teacher and friend. He knew the score ("I have no pull with any canonizing powers"), he refused to be humiliated, and he relied on facts and an occasional wry jab to set the story straight.

In fact, reading this collection of Jack's writings reminds me fully of his patience and good-humor as a teacher and a friend. I never saw much of his temper. He stated a point, waited for a reaction, and allowed the shit to fly with a little bit of a smile on his face. I have one glorious memory of a dinner party at his house where the conversation had turned to childbirth. At the end of a rambling back and forth among the guests, Jack, seated at the head of the dining room table, somehow got in the final word: "You have to eat the placenta!" To this day I marvel at his proclamation. I'd only hear that advice again twenty-five years later from a midwife, of course.

Jack's thinking was unique. He was a self-described Olsonite, but we know that there was a chemistry between him and Olson that went beyond a master-student relationship. His mind was intrinsically dexterous. Like Sherlock Holmes he always had immediate access to a repository of historical, anthropological, and theological fact, which he could combine and re-combine (Like he said in class, "Mythology is needed in places where lots of things are happening in order to arrange and understand reality") until he hit upon some useful and enlightening thought that then entered a poem or a conversation or a classroom lecture. It was partly his ability to relate the bigger picture of history to the little particulars of our lives that made him a great teacher. I remember him talking in one of our classes about vegetarianism (during that awful period when Reagan was still on the warpath with his late Cold War hijinks) and tossing out the observation "The Meat is pretty close to the Button." Sometime it took a while to get Jack's message—his statements could be brilliantly odd (for instance, "Most poets have their hand in the fire, but Warren Tallman has his hand in the ice cream blender"). There was other, more personal, shrink-like advice that he gave (again with that cheerful take it or leave it smile) that I still draw on today. Occasionally too, his subversive maneuvers were breathtaking. I'd give anything to revisit one of our class meetings during which Jack turned his attention to a couple of very square football players who sat in the back of the room. After some sly coaxing on Jack's part (as I remember it the words "psychedelics", "tripping", and "drugs" never entered the conversation) the jocks left the class nervously excited to seek out a dose of psilocybin mushrooms.

It's a pleasure to contemplate that shared Olsonian/Clarkeian trait of, for lack of a better term, "the opening of the field" (to borrow here from Robert Duncan)—that place where we embrace all of the possibilities of reality: non-linear space-time, dreamscapes, and even the things pushed toward the realm of conspiracy theory. The fact that a Google search produces no results for the phrase "the bicephalic mind" makes me pause to think about the gift of Jack's mentorship. Because we inevitably inhabit "the System" so-called, how can we think outside of it? (I hear the call for magic mushrooms for the entire football team.) In focusing on Olson, on Blake, on the Greeks, Jack asked his students to think bicephalically, to stand on two tracks, to let what we know and don't know co-mingle, to attend to myth and reality side-by-side as reality, to take clues from the Spicerian unseen in order to make sense of the real. In so-called rational circles all this talk is useless, and likewise the poet's work is dismissed. What do we do with Jack's anecdote of Olson saying "Santa Claus is a true god"? or with filmmaker Stan Brakhage's insistent refrain in the classroom and in interviews: "I believe in fairies, and elves, and demons"?

For me, a return to Jack's writing comes as a gift and as a reminder that couched inside of the propositions of poets are all of the things that "the System" would like to conveniently sweep under the rug. When Jack casually invokes "his lady in Dallas with the white luggage" in "The Metaphysics of Survival" I'm awake again, like I was in his classroom nearly thirty years ago. I imagine he regrets not making it into the twenty-first century, our ecological and political last act. (It must have seemed bizarre to some of my classmates when Jack suggested that the year 2160 (give or take a few decades) could see the end of the polar ice.)

If there's something about Jack's work that's hard to parse, it comes in the fact that these kinds of propositions raise more questions than they answer. We're left with the reminder that there's more to reality than the received information of the media and technology we subscribe to and even depend on for a cheap thrill. When I think of Jack's take on all of this, I can't reach for an affirmation of the poetical genius or a call to the masses to crush the system. I can hear him picking out a line from Allen Ginsberg's 1988 Charles Olson Memorial Lecture: "Nothing lasts forever . . . maybe we're on the way out."

Los Americans

Mike & Pat!

I am a flying saucer believe it or not I woke up
this morning to find myself just that strange
as it may seem at first hearing nonetheless
that's what I am and what is even stranger
is I saw you are too whether you know it
or not we both are now I don't know what
the social consequences of this discovery will be
whether we will roll down the hills together
like Easter Eggs or just what we will be able
to do together or what our flight pattern will be
whether we want to talk as much as we do
or keep more silent or what I do know we will
think of something more interesting than standing
on the head of a pin not exactly our cup of tea.

Jack

July 23, 1971

[Jack Clarke to Al [Mike] and Pat Glover]

LOTS OF DOOM

The Canton Reading, December 12, 1971
—*After thy Charles, fair*

"I personally like the ultimate freedom of being unknown."
—John Matus

I DON'T KNOW, I'VE GOT SEVERAL BEGINNINGS but the one I brought is really what it comes down to, I suppose you're all subscribers to your own house organ right?[1] That letter, to see that again was a knockout. But I hadn't heard the name of the place really because Al kind of hits us more upstate New York with the Chinese affirmation, he calls it Canton. And yet in our own activity in publishing the last few years we've been relying upon Lawrence so heavily that . . . but I hadn't realized until . . . and I hope that doesn't offend the memory of the other guy that you probably know better than I do—but I heard via Saint Lawrence[2] as Saint Lawrence and like that was the Lawrence that was more than the other one, except from inference, from William Carlos Williams's *In The American Grain*, where he tries to get to the source of the American experience. But at that time—this[3] is copyright 1923, and 1950, by Frieda Lawrence—that's prior to that, right? *In The American Grain* is '27.

But instantly before we left the house coming up—yeah, coming up north. It's funny to come back, you know—you're going north and then turn around and think you're coming toward home but it's really still north by the compass in his vehicle which is an International Scout.[4] So it may be off that much. I don't know as there is any way to do it internationally.

But just before we left . . . see I've got a poem that begins with the word pre.[5] It's really just three, three movements of a . . . well I don't know how long 'cause I got stuck on nine, but I didn't know it because eight didn't seem right. So this is one, two, three,[6] and I don't know how far it's going to go. Maybe not much more because this three really . . . I mean I did these three as themselves and then the other seven that I proposed to run from them were really days later and a kind of exegesis of the material contained in the first three. But I don't know what any of it is about or what it means or anything about it.

As we left the house I looked at a poster[7] that I'd never seen before of Charles Olson, and a poem that, really . . . I mean it's for the new Maximus poems[8] which come after the volume called IV, V, VI.[9] Well, his man—the man he invented—was called Maximus. So Maximus said, (or is it thought)?—He said . . . he is in fact pre, or prior, to the depths, or in the next line before the sources of things, prior to that. I mean he was born before there were depths or sources, dig? So that's what I think these things are about, but they're new to me, and I've no really discursive sense that I could even articulate any of that. So what I have got is a book which is.

I took a sabbatical in 1970 and spent most of it in Oregon. When I was there I was asked to furnish materials that would constitute a full issue of a magazine called *Fathar*.[10] There had been two prior to this and this is *Fathar* III. I think the first had been in English or Arabic and then . . . let me see, what's the other numeral system before . . . let's see, the third is Roman but before the . . . like Lawrence says he's Roman rather than Celtic in his attention to what he calls system—did you all read that letter carefully? I mean it's such a beauty. But what's the other system for? Well, I guess the first one was letters—anyone remember? —like o-n-e for one, and then the second was Arabic. So I don't know what he's going to do with four, but I got stuck with . . . he's a Fellini fan, and so I got stuck with, at that moment, *Satyricon*. He had sent me this other picture on *Fathar* 2, the back of . . . it's Marcello. Remember that movie where he's sitting on the back of the cart and it's like, "shoot louder"—that movie, "I can't hear the shots." This guy up in the attic who answers him telepathically, with firecrackers. He can neither speak nor, yah he hears but he doesn't speak and so he answers everything that Marcello says with the fire, the rhythm of firecrackers. And they go off, so at the end when he's finally made it with the woman of his choice and they're leaving in this automobile down the strip he thinks he hears a shot, firecracker, so he stops the car and everything and gets out, goes over, and that's when he delivers that line that Duncan had on the back of #2, "Shoot louder, I can't hear the," something—not music, but not shots either. I don't know . . . I can't, not because he can't hear it, it fades away.

And so another way of saying there's a source for something is to call it unknown, which I've been calling . . . if you can hear that the way Lawrence has it in another place, the place we were working from when we finished the last plate of the last *Magazine of Further Studies*.[11] We had gone to Lawrence in this plate, so it's '17' is it? It's a war piece, probably some month of 1916 or '17 isn't it? '18? 1918. And he calls it, carefully, the "unknowen unknowen".

I'm from the mid-west,[12] as John Temple tells me, so there's this problem of making it like Old English, you know, because in contemporary pronunciation it is one—"knowen" is one syllable, like known, real quick. But I'm still doing my own speech, which is knowen . . . so if I say "unknowen," you can hear, it sounds ridiculous with this Englishman because he's—I'll try to say it, "the unknown unknown". So if you know that you don't know you might say that it was the unknown unknown.[13] But don't hear unknown as some place that's vague because you don't know about it, it's used carefully as: not the opposite but the contrary of the known. The known is a place, the unknown is a place. And if you want to say anything further, then you have to say even better than that nice reduplication, which we'll get to.

Some of the poems in here are looking that way because, for some reason, it's a very particular fix that I have on these materials that to some extent I share with Olson. This reduplication comes up a lot like the "barbar" in barbarian and the "tartar" in the Tartars, and the Tartar Relation.

There are some dog poems in here. I mean, I never particularly dug dogs. Some guy wrote to me and said, "That's a pretty weird ally to choose."[14] I hadn't even thought of that. But there they are. What I did during the sabbatical was to trust what was happening and try to keep an accurate journal. So I didn't know until much later the connections with that. In fact I didn't know 'til last night's paper that the dog population has increased from the thirties, which was something like a couple hundred thousand, less than half a million, and today they figure a million and a half licensed, but probably more than two million on the street. I didn't even have that kind of enthusiasm about dogs at that moment. It turned out that . . . what I'm trying to get to is his first paragraph which begins "As a matter of fact".[15] One fact was that . . . I guess it's two facts really. I'll give you one, see if you think it's the same or it's another, if it's two.

Maybe you know the story, from the Tartar Relation, the husbands of the wives were dogs?[16] And then you know the other fact, it might be the same fact, but it's the one on "hound," the etymological fact of hound or hund, like Atilla the Hun and that thing. You probably know that better as a sociological reference to Zen. Ask him,[17] he's working on Tokharian. That's the fact that there's an etymological congruence that will get you, if you're very very very careful, somewhat ahead geographically.

Well that runs out there, in a way. That's still school. I want to stay on this unknown thing. There's kind of a literary history to it which probably coincides with the later history, since the Second World War anyway, of the little magazine. Well, that's still school business though isn't it?

Well the poster that I looked at as I left really says it, that the man I went to school with—the figure of his imagination tells him (and now that he's not there to be told—he tells us) what he was before or prior to the origins, the sources. And yet this book that I can even—I've never read it—I read it myself but I haven't read it as a "reading ." So this is what I'm really interested in finding out, what it says. And I have an idea that it has most to say, not in contradiction to what Maximus is telling you, but prior to that, it's fathomed in an order of things, like Pip falling off the boat or something. It's not . . . I mean I have to do that because it's what I've stuck myself with, to fathom. So I'm going to do that just to see what it is saying. Yet I don't want anybody to think that it's putting up itself as like a return to.

So I began with *In the American Grain* because I think that is the necessary step that a student has to make. But once that's made I don't want any . . . see if I'm going to speak about the unknown, which I want to speak about, I don't want that to be confused with school, where you would do the other operation, hopefully with guidance. This is a "reading" situation, and my own situation I want to be unknown rather than ahead of itself. You know what I mean? School is always ahead of itself. You graduate to a condition that you don't experience perhaps 'til years later. Or like Olson said it—maybe one soliloquy will stick in the ear of a dentist, but he might not hear it 'til he's pulled a lot of teeth. But no matter what your later profession might be, you remember, eventually you remember.

I don't know what to call this other activity, mainly because we haven't—since that last magazine when we ended up with Lawrence —we really haven't taken the next step. We took one kind of falteringly public step in Vancouver,[18] but it wasn't the step we'd perhaps like to have taken. But what we got straight was we were four guys. We weren't allowed to appear together. We had to do it like each—you know, single. So we got that straight, with our wives kind of breathlessly waiting in the wings ready to follow any other kind of misadventure that might occur, before or after.

So we did that, but I think we kind of left it in '69. In fact, the meeting was here, which is nice, but it was not Saint Lawrence then it was still "Canton," you know, it wasn't quite, 'cause school's a hard thing to get to once you've left it. Our last line was "so play",[19] which fitted in real well with that particular year because everybody was thinking that. I think that this next year really for us and for everyone will have to do with this thing I'm calling the unknown, in Lawrence's sense, in that the '60's was.

Well let me backtrack it just a little bit with a story, because history's hard to get straight without a story right ahead of it. And that's what this pre business is about, like before the source, not before but born before. It's important to remember that that's the principle. Not, you know, not any kind of . . . no hedge in that, no hedge, just born before.

Well, in the time we've just experienced, now we can call it the '60's, the story that hits me is the . . . well I don't really have to go into the mythology[20] of it, but there's a point in the life of a marriage when the woman, after—and the man—after many terms of a happy marriage, there comes a time when the woman asks the man where he came from. As simple as that. And it's the one question that she never was [supposed] to ask. But over the years, or over the whatever, she couldn't—it had been so, or had gotten so, blissful that she couldn't not ask. And the moment she asks he has to tell her. In fact he so much has to tell her that he tells her many many times not to ask. But when it comes time, she does. So he has to answer. And it's a hard answer, but it's one that is up I think. I think the '60's were . . . the kind of sense that we all have from having survived them, and not everybody did . . . was the return to the earth itself in all its expressions, whether communal or a re-interest in the things of the earth, its clothing, its fruit. The range of mundane expression of that, so that people were interested again in objects. I think that that was accomplished by woman and that's what she was able to tell, given her own responsibility. Now it's called Women's Lib. That she was able to tell, more than tell—I mean strongly tell, demand—that that was where the attention should be placed, and a man was forced to be less and less abstract about his, Lawrence would say, "touch". It did make a difference how he petted the cat or lighted his cigarette or whatever. The chauvinism was that ingrained, that's what has gradually come out, that it was a very deep thing.

I don't want to dwell on that because I think we've all . . . I mean I don't think it matters a bit if you're married or if you're not. Marriage is simply . . . I don't mean to be school again, but it's a strategy or an invention—the Elizabethans called them Dainty Devices when they circulated them amongst themselves and wrote sonnets. But a human invention, literally a human invention that would make it possible for a man and for a woman to take hold of their own time, take hold of their own times, their own souls. Some way of getting a hold of it and living their life and no other, which was indiscriminate and all the other phrases of indiscretion that you can think of, because it lacked a continuity. So it's invention that allows, or makes it possible for, two people to live. I think the responsibility of that was picked up and reenacted in the '60's, which is wonderful when you read *In the American Grain*, because it's what Dr. Williams was so . . . having seen so many patients was . . . he was really ready for that.

I think the '70s are just the contrary of that. That earth context having been provided and the attention shifted the man is now being asked to provide the other half of this thing called marriage. I think his responsibility is this thing I'm calling the unknown. If the point was to know the earth context, and I don't mean simply in the sense that you'd have to read The Whole Earth Catalogue, its description or tabulation or anything like that, but just the fact that you weren't so easily able to, well, touch, keep going back to that, to Lawrence's word. To touch things quite, as Olson says so "jauntily," to treat your distinction from the animal quite so jauntily. So you have a lot of reassertion of anima, animal something, animism? I don't like it. I don't think that's it. We don't have a term for it. It's a concern with the animate, Olson calls "the animate,"[21] that's probably as good as any way to say animal. A non-human animate expression, which Charles got from the earth itself, and poets like, for example, McClure was a lion and, you know, Gary Snyder. Well, I mean, you could go on, but that's again literary history.

It is now the man's responsibility to provide, in speech, the unknown. And he doesn't know what it is either, so I think what he does is invent it. The best story that might foreshadow the '70's refocus now on the adversary situation that we've got ourselves into with the legal structure, I mean the whole system of laws is anomalous. A guy told me last night anomalous was meaning there's no *nomoi*,[22] and he's a Greek scholar, but that's Greek, that word for what they call real love, a thing you abide by.

I was at the zoo a couple of weeks ago and I said "That gorilla's gonna get that guy," because every time he comes by the cage he hits him in the arm. About three days later in the evening paper, the gorilla named Samson got this guy. Already, took three days from the time I just looked over and said, "He's obviously going to get him because he doesn't dig it." He'd just look out—he'd leave his arm but he'd never look at the guy. He'd jab him you know or . . . like Gary Snyder said, I think, that he would be happy to be eaten by a wolf, if he was dead.

What I'm trying say is: even though I don't know what it is, I know what it's not. So don't think that if there's a dog in there it's a dog totem or something. I mean keep it as weird as it is. It's at least as weird as these husbands of the Amazons, if we're talking marriage that is. And if that possibility was accomplished in the '60's, if there's anything for a man to do next it's to invent what it is he's going to say. Because he has to tell where, or what . . . no I think it's better where he's from, where he comes from, the origin of it.

I know a couple of stories that are pretty close, but the best one is a story from . . . it's American but it's probably South American. I've forgotten the name of the tribe.[23] This guy was charged with being a shaman, making this girl sick, and that was his crime. His defense was primarily himself—he did have counsel—was not to plead innocent, which he was, but to not do a thing, to merely invent the reason he did it. Because his counsel told him: "You're not going to get off. You're guilty, everybody is, whatever you're charged with." So he says, "Well,

if that's it, I'm going to have a hard time, but I'll have a go at it." So
he invents this story, like he says: "Well, I kind of picked it up on the
side." And the elders said, "No, it's not picked up that way." And they
keep saying "no" because they know and he doesn't. And all the people
of the village are watching—it's a three-way reinforcement: the guy, the
court, and the Society. And they all want the same thing to win, but he
doesn't know what it is. And the people know 'cause they're the folk,
and the court knows because it knows, so they're all together in this
thing and nobody can get out of it. As the burden of guilt increases he
keeps inventing and he invents 'til he really is getting into it. He says
his great grandfather was a shaman, that it was transmitted to . . . and
he became a shaman in that normal way which he'd found out from the
previous non-story he was telling. He had the feathers or some amulets,
some objects on his wall to prove it. And they said, "Well, okay, we'll go
over to your house." He says, "Well, you can't tear my wall down. You'll
tear my whole house down." "Well, we're going over to your house to
see if you've got the stuff." So they started to tear down the walls and
everything.

At this point the story does get kind of vague, which shows you that
both society and the shaman, all three, and the other one, the author-
ity, the magistracy, in a Puritan like . . . they all agree about something
'cause they kind of give a little leeway, 'cause all of a sudden the stuff is
in his wall. And all the magistrates go "ohhh". I mean, they're knocked
out that this stuff is really there and they all look at each other, you
know, like that's it. And all the people are clapping and it's great. One
thing leads to another and this is the first credible proof that he's got,
but as it continues the court is more and more satisfied, and he is too
because he's finding out that what he's invented really is the truth. He
really is, obviously, a shaman. And so by proving that—whoever reports
the story is a French guy like Levi-Strauss[24]—whoever, in their system
of jurisprudence, who proves his own, through imagination, through
his own personal power of invention, who proves he actually . . . see,
their bind is that you might have committed a crime without actually
having been there, without knowing that you were committing it. So
they have to prove. What they're interested in is making an accord with
reality and the imagination. If you can prove that you in fact accom-
plished the so-called crime that they say you did, then it supports—or
as the anthropologists say, it collaborates—the system that they're inter-

ested in. Which he does, and in so doing is a shaman who goes over to the girl's house and instantly heals her. Not only does the system win, I mean, the whole thing does. And then he has his career, it's founded. Through his own inventiveness he was able to return to or reach his origins, although he didn't know them.

What I'm saying is that the marriage dynamic has become that way, that when it's asked of you, you must come up with it. Not come up with the known—that will be rejected every time because that's what's just happened—but the unknown which you don't know. But you must complete that half in order to fulfill your responsibility as the custodian of that place. Which then would get us to the two things that you'd . . . like, the '60's or the '70's. That earth and that heaven . . . being able to treat that time as vertical, not simply sequential, but turning it up on its end so that you can see where you've been, and because where you've been follows something, something follows it.

So I know that what he says is true, on the poster, but that doesn't mean that it's not exactly where I have to work . . . or anyone who's there has to work to be able to pick it up. In other words, pick up what the actual question, the actual demand is, that you must answer.

It's kind of draggy, you know, it's like that knowledge, what you know school-wise, will always be ahead—you'll always know more. The burden of the '60's, at least as Olson presented them, and I think I can use him 'cause I think he's the furthest instance of the '60's. (That's kind of a private term of ours—further.) Just think of the future then, I mean the next step that you might take. He did that because he was able to sit down. He had that kind of a metabolism perhaps. He could do his dancing sitting down, and I think that that's true, that's simply true. But I think we'll be able to answer the phone maybe or move around a little bit because of that fact, that we know that he's sitting there, I mean, that a man could do it. Creeley said that what he found interesting about Olson's death was that a man could die. That was new to him, you know, it hadn't happened before in his experience. Probably hadn't happened since the Civil War or something, that a man could do that. Because, like Lawrence said, "marriage is further than death". Like the North Country letter, he won't stop at that image of the crucifixion and leave it at that. He must go on to the next plate and the next plate and the next. It's being really, married or not, it's being able to see that there is a new . . . I haven't got a word for it yet . . . but a new unknown. It's an unknown something. It's a thing that must be and yet it's only there if you do it.

Well, Lawrence. And I mean I'll just read without any bibliog . . . . okay it's that book.[25]

> As a matter of fact, unless a woman is held, by man, safe within the bounds of belief, she becomes inevitably a destructive force. She can't help herself. A woman is almost always vulnerable to pity. She can't bear to see anything physically hurt. But let a woman loose from the bounds and restraints of man's fierce belief, in his gods and in himself, and she becomes subtly diabolic. The colossal evil of the united spirit of Woman. WOMAN, German woman or American woman,

his wife is German

> or every other sort of woman, in the last war, was something frightening. As every man knows.

> . . . Unless a man believes in himself and his gods, genuinely: unless he fiercely obeys his own Holy Ghost; his woman will destroy him. Woman is the nemesis of doubting man. She can't help it.

> . . . Revenge! REVENGE! It is this that fills the unconscious spirit, of woman today. Revenge against man, and against the spirit of man which has betrayed her into unbelief. Even when she is most sweet and a Salvationist, she is her most devilish, is woman. She gives her man the sugar-plum . . . And when he's taken this sugar-plum in his mouth, a scorpion comes out of it . . . She will have it,

he's just said woman and her revenge again

> She will have it, and go on having it, for decades and decades, unless she's stopped. And to stop her you've got to believe in yourself and your gods, your own Holy Ghost, Sir Man; and then you've got to fight her, and never give in. She's a devil. But in the long run she is conquerable. And just a tiny bit of her wants to be conquered. You've got to fight three-quarters of her, in absolute hell, to get at the final quarter of her that wants a release, at last, from the hell of her own revenge. But it's a long last. And not yet.

And whatever that date is . . . so he's writing that in the '20's, before the dog population was even . . . and then he goes on to say some other things that are less abstract, things that are unreadable, but in the next chapter he gets to what I've found out, and that's weird, to be the thing that this book was about, but I didn't know it then.

And he's talking about Pearl. Remember Pearl, who's the daughter, the offspring of Hester and Dimmesdale? You all know *The Scarlet Letter*. I keep going back to school. It must be the . . . maybe I'll stand up to read.

Maybe I've left out something that's crucial, the fact that Lawrence has said, and you scholars correct me, that if you sin against the Father and the Son you're forgiven, both times, but if you sin against the Holy Ghost you're in trouble. Is that right? That's what Lawrence says prior to this. And when he's speaking before, he's speaking of whence man or woman, that's why I'm belaboring his point of ourselves and Mr. Lawrence and what we have to do with each other. It wasn't always that a woman was granted that possibility. I mean that's all I wanted to say. That's what Lawrence is talking about when he says the Pearl. But he's in that date, that's how many years ago, a long time, like he says "not yet".

> There is only one penalty: the loss of his own integrity. Man should never do the thing he believes to be wrong. Because if he does, he loses his own singleness, wholeness, natural honour.
>
> If you want to do a thing, you've either got to believe, sincerely, that it's your true nature to do this thing—or else you've got to let it alone.
>
> . . . if you doubt, abstain.
>
> A thing that you sincerely believe in cannot be wrong, because belief does not come at will. It comes only from the Holy Ghost. . . . Therefore a thing you truly believe in cannot be wrong.
>
> But there is such a thing as spurious belief. There is such a thing as evil belief: a belief that one cannot do wrong.

Have you ever had that? Has anybody in this room ever had that?

> There is also such a thing as half-spurious belief. And this is the rottenest of all. The devil lurking behind the cross.

Which is what Ed Sanders's book called *The Family* exposes—exactly that, the devil lurking behind the cross. Does that sound about right? That's what he found out, that's what his investigation—he had private eyes and everything—that's what he found out it was lurking behind. How many of you have read William Blake to know how that evil lurks behind the cross formula? Blake right? Well that's a long time ago. Long before history.

> So there you are. Between genuine belief, and spurious belief, and half-genuine belief, you're as likely as not to be in a pickle.

> Hester and Dimmesdale believed in the Divine Father, and almost gloatingly sinned against Him . . . .

> Pearl no longer believes in the Divine Father. She says so. She has no Divine Father. Disowns Papa both big and little.

> So she can't sin against him.

> What will she do, then, if she's got no god to sin against? Why, of course, she'll not be able to sin at all. She'll go her own way gaily, and do as she likes, and she'll say, afterwards, when she's made a mess: "Yes, I did it. But I acted for the best, and therefore I am blameless. It's the other person's fault. Or else it's Its fault."

> She will be blameless, will Pearl, come what may.

> And the world is simply a string of Pearls today. And America is a whole rope of these absolutely immaculate Pearls, who can't sin, let them do what they may, because they've no god to sin against. Mere men, one after another. Men with no ghost to their name.

> Pearls!

> Oh, the irony, the bitter, bitter irony of the name! Oh, Nathaniel, you great man! Oh, America, you Pearl, you Pearl without a blemish!

> How can Pearl have a blemish, when there's no one but herself to judge Herself? Of course she'll be immaculate, even if, like Cleopatra, she drowns a lover a night in her dirty Nile. The Nilus Flux of her love.

> By Hawthorne's day it was already Pearl. Before swine, of course. There never yet was a Pearl that wasn't cast before swine.

> It's part of her game, part of her pearldom.

> Because when Circe lies with a man, he's a swine after it, if he wasn't one before. Not she. Circe is the great white impeccable Pearl.

And yet, oh, Pearl, there's a Nemesis even for you.

There's a Doom, Pearl.

Doom! What a beautiful northern word. Doom.

The doom of the Pearl.

Who will write that Allegory?

I thought, I will! Quick, it must be there.

Well, it goes on and on, but that's as far as I got. And it must be something like that, although the only poem in it, on it, was rejected by the editor. So I don't know whatever happened to the ceiling, it was like one of those Pearls in the . . . you had one, I think, fall down, but this was just a tiny little hole where there was a mouse (see Appendix A). But there is a mouse finally at the end, comes in here, but there's another mouse that this Pearl was given to 'cause . . . I'm not using it to put anything down, I mean, you got to hear that the Pearl is still the Pearl in the sense you know it from The Pearl of Medieval Romance and you know all the way to, who is it, Steinbeck? Is that the most recent narrative of Pearl?[26]

So with that extended context—it was a long time. It's a full hour of context. Let's do something, then we'll just start fresh, okay? That's school—now we'll do the other thing.

—Intermission—

DURING THAT SABBATICAL YEAR, 1970, it begins in Buffalo, in a place called Delaware and it moves to, kind of on the way, the second section is Oregon, where we stayed most of the summer. And then there's a coming back procession and it gets to another Buffalo residence or, no, it gets to the holidays. Then it was a residence called Oxford— Oxford, New York, where we were briefly, and then back to Buffalo with a residence called Sheridan Transit for two months and then a residence called Mariner for two months and finally, by May, having left in May the first time. It goes from Memorial Day to Memorial Day, those are the two dates—I mean that's the beginning and the end. Then the last was the residence we had finally gotten to which was the tenth residence in Buffalo which means that there were six before the one that this picks up at which is called Delaware.

I can read the . . . well, it's like a tribute to an anonymous poet, an Anglo-Saxon poet, of a rune poem, and it bridges it with the theoretical stuff that I was giving you from that first hour on the known and the unknown and to what Lawrence calls the "Doom of the Pearl". And having done that then I'll make a selection from each one of these passages and then, if you want, we could take another selection.[27] But let's go through it once and see if I can hit one each time, that first, the pre condition, goes like this:

> property is solace to everyone

I better start again 'cause this is my translation via my wife via somebody else, like the guy who punctuated the book. So I don't know as I could, or would, claim the translation, but I've got to, you see, and like the book itself, since there's no way for me to break these things. I mean they come and go. They just start and stop. They're non-punctuated, there's no punctuation. There's an occasional period, that's it.

> property is solace to everyone of men
> however each of men shall
> deal much if he will for the Lord
> to cast lots of doom

So there's a piece in here which was written before this called LOTS OF VESTURE. You see it's untitled because it's a magazine really; it's not a book. If it were, I think that it would feel right to have it called Lots simply Lots. So then there's kind of a thing, that Memorial Day thing that I got from Lewis MacAdams, whom you know from his having read here.[28]

He got back from Egypt and told me a wild story—several—but one that really hit. He was in the tombs, in the burial chambers, and he discovered that the pictures weren't from the Book of the Dead, they weren't transformative or initiatory sequences of pictures. They were all scenes from everyday life. I told that to Sanders the night before last and he said "Who was being hyped then?" And I was kind of at a loss, but I thought, "Only the people who usually are." If marriage is further than death, you know where that leaves anyone who is waiting to die for the privilege of Heaven or any of those other designations. It works both ways you know: it might be a boon or a complete drag.

Well anyway it was that sense of it that Lewis gave me a completely new take on, you know, grouse or something. It was really just . . . really ordinary, normal, as those men had at a certain point. If you do find out that you are before the source of things, you discover that there wasn't any. I mean at some actual point in your life you can terminate that kind of school. And so, that you did it. And that's what these big monumental things in stone, which are ways of making sure that the earth is reinstated at the end. Not that he's trying to take the stuff with him, but since every initiatory procedure is to bring the person more into the world, that final one is likewise his final, and for the spectators equally the last and most beautiful chance to come in, and he's got all the reminders there. I mean he's literally got his stuff with him. And I knew that, theoretically, but I didn't know it from a traveller's point of view—I haven't travelled that much. I've never been out of America and that shows in this thing too. It's a kind of . . . I don't know what it is, so I'll just read that. It's called "We are the Gypsies of Coal Sack Bluff". And so, it's one of those splits, it begins:

We are the Gypsies
        painted gypsum Themis men
        pure white chalk cliffs
        my Grandfather used to take us
        fishing from out of the box
        came all contents needed
        Egypt likewise Lewis found
        his home with nobles painted
        scenes from Every Day Life
        my piano too will be covered
        with the dust

                of Coalsack Bluff

I read that in a dentist's office. I mean, I got the Coalsack Bluff from a dentist.

That's the departure, and I was going to leave my piano in a sculptor's studio. He was going to plaster the room so that my piano would then, in a year's accumulation of dust, be covered.

So the opening poem was written January 23rd, 1970. It's really a recital of my last meeting with Olson on the night before Easter of '69. And which then turned out to be our last night and it's called THE CHALLENGE. It opens with a quatrain, a four, a four lane highway, yeah, a four line thing from . . . this would be a, or is, I should say, North-western Crow or maybe Raven, depending upon your State. This is like British Columbia or maybe a little further, I mean pretty North, almost Eskimo, but still Indian.

So I wouldn't know how to pronounce it, I mean, the first thing is one of those redoubles like Tartar or Berber. This is like caw caw, only they spell it Qoaxqoax, or you could read it coax coax. As Olson said to me, "It's never pushed from behind or pulled from ahead but coaxed from within."

And so coax always seemed like a nice . . . you know, but it's, I don't know, a little too feminine or something. So I usually, usually? I only read it once. I say co ax co ax ooalanoo. It's

> Qoaxqoaxualanu Xsiwae
> Sat by the Door
> And there was a Woman
> Rooted in the Floor

And that's where it picks up. Charles always made a big thing of having the seal of Black Mountain for his doorstop. It was right there. Right there.

And this has to go fast 'cause it's like a syntax of disorder and it's mostly telephone, if you can get that credit card thing done away with. And like he's not the challenge, nor is marriage the challenge, or anything like that. It's like the challenge of . . . today it feels like the challenge of the unknown.

If the '60's were to reify the known, the '70's are to reify the unknown, which is a different thing. So you have, there's only one thing left to do and that's invent. Charles always told us that if we were to be of any use we had to be patented, not copyrighted. As an institute I mean. You got an institute, he wasn't interested in anything less than, like Leary said that night "the men behind the machines" (and it sounded like everybody because there's that sense of being literally behind the machine). Well, that's another piece, I think, maybe later, when we find out more about it, what the Human Universe is. To make a careful distinction between human and those other things like machines and other realms of nature. I think that three of the clearest men are Blake, Lawrence, and Olson, on what it is to be human and nothing else, simply that. Or simply that that's the trouble: with no punctuation you've got to rely I think on inflection. Okay this is a phone:

raging through the house
you never saw me that way
he said he was trying to
tell me something I hadn't
heard previously the night

we stood in his backyard under
the stars the conversation
of another his mother hadn't
given him what mine had he
pointed out the lights two
doors down beckoned as did

the other four he said he
had going or ventured there
was no other way to have
such a conversation now
that he had gone and got

himself in such a way the
way he was That Night I
said If you speak to Her
She will speak to you because

that was my experience but
he shook his head and looked
at me incredulously as though
a distant memory of a world
long ago departed had intruded

upon our conversation was
something about quality or
the simplicity of my situation
the Triangle was of no use
to him it had come down to

this or these five impossible
so when the phone rang these
many months later it was all
of a sudden Kate and the wife
she must have been to him Blake

> he said Creeley once had tried
> to write it The Island names
> like John and Mary his life
> was over That Night the morning
> after I couldn't cry looked out
>
> and said There's an ocean out
> there and he said yes but
> then upon more careful
> consideration said
> Actually it's a bay

Well it's . . . I could think of a million other ways to read that, but, you know, it's like impossible to, like it says, it should be in French but it's not, you know. It's that impossible.

So that gets us out of New York and the first thing in Oregon was this . . . thing. It's really simple, it's from being in . . . when I was in the first grade, being in the marriage play of Tom Thumb. They have a marriage ceremony and we were married in Holy Padlock, and then at the end of the thing, the whole thing happened and we were raised, and this girl was the girl next door, whose name was Joy, and we were raised in a basket. So that's all this is:

> I wish I could say my initiation
> that's all I needed right there
> began in the First Grade when
> I played Tom Thumb and was raised
> up in a basket with Joy to the
> ceiling where I unhooked the Stars
> & Stripes from the nail on which
> they had caught while the whole
> school sang God Bless America
> I can

See I took the maybe out.[29] Well it seems that's where the America, that's what that thing is about, but that's where it begins, I feel it really. That's what it's really saying, but maybe it isn't. Then, I'll just read the poem. Then back home. Duncan [McNaughton]'s got them in the wrong order. He did a little bit of juggling. I think I'll just go right back from the coast to this little town called Oxford and do this dog poem. I'll do two of them.

Gee, it's gone. He really did change things a little bit. Well maybe I'll just have to do one called OXFORD GONE TO THE DOGS. Where's GONE TO THE DOGS? DOGS VIEW FAR FROM IT, I've got that. I don't think this other one, did he leave it out, you think? It's here? Oh, here it is. This is the bad one I wanted to go directly to. OXFORD GONE TO THE DOGS, not America but:

OXFORD GONE TO THE DOGS

Each of the houses now
is guarded by a dog
or dogs the original reads
even some that aren't
only have the sign
to frighten others more
fortunate who can afford
the actual that is
there are places between
where houses stand
sometimes unprotected
but the dogs' territories
extend to cover the
entire neighborhood is
made of these lines
of urine obvious when
pissed in snow but
even in the dark will
know when crossed
the changes in uproar
so noticeable the
new ring of voices
the people let them go
out walking you are
constantly aware beware
the automobile has made
easier to go through

Then it switches JOB ONLY GOES THROUGH. And then I heard that just today in the Lawrence Letter. If you read that one:

JOB ONLY GOES THROUGH

Looking neither to the
right nor left he walks
chiefly down the avenue
cutting directly through
all lines of yellow piss
which have no meaning to
him The German Shepherd
of Oxford quietly returns
home in the hush not even
a yip out of the big Black
One the Ugly One

Coming home from there, back to Buffalo, this will be that next place
which is Sheridan Transit and looking, spending all that time looking.
This is called:

A CRYPTIC EMERGENCY

inhabits the world as I
see it the Red & the Black
& the Great White Light
streams through broken
branches the Lake Itself
a swirl of broken Ice
there is no other but this
One Stark Naked

And around that same time this sort of funny one:

PURCHASE ORDER THE STATE OF NEW YORK NELSON ROCKYFELLER GOVENOR

We need 10 big Red Rolls Royces
to pick us up and they need us
to pick them up see how it could
work David wouldn't have to go
to the hospital every morning he
could be picked up and taken else
where in the city or country we

wouldn't have to neglect each
other as we do because we don't
simply have the means of getting
about in this snow we need a rest-
oration of Muspil we need 10 big
Red Rolls Royces would restore
this City

That's old fashioned, I mean, you know, and when we finally got to this place called Mariner, I'll read one, maybe two. I'll read this one called:

LOTS OF VESTURE

the reapportionment of the body as
a city filled with people coming &
going my dream of the Queene is no
blood shed red car streaking over
Skyway to Elm St ramp to come out
at Plaza where the looters see her
turn the corner all eyes glued to
her weave all traffic stopped the
windows reflect the red and green
lots of vesture

And this one called BREAD ALONE. That's an old jazz term:

for now each day is a communion
the earthen table set by Isis
for The Man Who Died (this is
for Gerrit Lansing Solar Knight
of Gloucester Massachusetts his
house a blaze of afternoon glory)
for who knows the value of humanity
is not in silver & gold except by
traditional East of Eden standard
for Adonais lives in Southern Comfort

I mean I was thinking of Janis[30] you know. So then there's this SHAKES SONNET which . . . we had these shakes, they call them shakes on the wall, pasted in . . . and this particular thing was how to get out of there. So we did, and I won't even read it. So that's Mariner.

And then we went home to the house we finally found after all that looking. In other words, a couple of things. He's got one out of place here but, well, I'll read this one. This is for a piano player, really an acquaintance of mine, used to play with Miles, Wynton Kelly.[31] It is called:

AND ALL THE DARK PLACE WERE LIGHTED UP
FOR WYNTON

Basking in the limelight the Green Knight
re-enters his summer abode All flames gold
as the day Loki made All definite wonders
of the invisible world take on the look of
day-time curtains that Anger will in time
produce the Wolf that this harrowing will
replace that howling & the Seven Sleepers
awake to find their initiatic cosmos fully
homologized by 'talk' which is only a par-
ticular case of how to entertain those who
recline on one elbow waiting for the next
blast find themselves the players of such
Trump the limit of hesitation is a Major
Third the Tenth chord he gave up in the
vaguer hope of tracing the Queene is All.

The mythology of that story is Lancelot, when he finally . . . and he does, he does do it like a man would and she is not at all impressed. He thinks she'll be, you know, the whole thing, and then she says "I don't even want to see that guy." He says "What do you mean, he just saved you from Hell." She says, "I don't want to see him. He's the draggiest guy I've ever laid eyes on." And so he finally gains an audience some-how. Probably 'cause they were married or something. And the next day he does get an audience with her and she says "I saw you hesitate those two full steps."

See, he was summoned in a cart and the cart was moving and the cart said "okay". He was immediately supposed to get in, but he hesitated that much. Old Gawain just took one look and said, "This isn't my trip." He took the sword over the water, cutting his fingers, and it was awful, but he wanted that. The worst possibility was he could fall in the water and his armour would fill up and he'd be sunk. But this other guy chose this thing like trial by fire and it was, you know, a different one. And the guy I read, who was Zimmer,[32] says it was the more difficult one of the two. I mean Lancelot's was. So I like Gawain myself, but anyway he's got that far. In his system of discipline, I suppose you receive it in school as Courtly Love, and also someone like this other guy I told you about, a more primitive so-called training program.

Over the years you're preparing for that speech you've got to make when the figure like The Devouring Ghost[33] or Lawrence's ghost, you're own soul, asks you to say something and she's there and she has a map and she erases half of it and you have to instantly complete the other half in order to escape being instantly scarfed by her. In both these traditions a man prepares for such a thing throughout his life so that when this time comes, he's not at a loss. That's what I mean by the known, that you might complete the map at that moment.

The unknown is a situation more like where you have to complete the map and just as quickly, but you haven't prepared for it as such. You literally don't know what to do, but you must do something. And so I keep coming back to that word invention, Blake's sense of invention[34] rather than fiction. But what do you do? You make it up. That's all. I mean what else could you do? Don't tell any girls that.

It's like, Lawrence writes that to a girl and at the end of the letter . . . no, to a lady . . . and says "Don't show this to anybody. This is only for the good." So THE DECADE IS COMPLETE. No:

THE DECADE IS COMPLETE

> I can prove it one night in Santa Fe
> she jumped up on the bed collapsed
> the springs & all getting away from
> the little mouse who had entered the
> room she wouldn't stay there insisted
> we sleep outside which we did after
> much grumbling nay is all ye need to
> know

It's like that, you know! So except for a kind of tribute to the man behind the scene, which in the book is called . . . this is really the last poem, but Duncan, the editor, put it in this place. It was written I think at that spot called Mariner and it's called:

THE WARDER OF THE WOOD

You've used your mind but you haven't
used your body he said as he sickled
off my private parts with one ancient
sweep of hand our nice correspondence
he had earlier noted & we had trusted
to come true as in the picture he took
finally what happened was the twin 1/2s
of our Identity were fused to the tune
of loud cymbals clashing so when it was
time to leave one another it was simply
a matter of separating the two he had
thus made

I don't read that very good. I mean I don't know how to read it. There's a million zaps going on in there that a . . . syntactically I mean. But it's very ordinary. All the fact is is the touch you know that is further than death. That's all. And that's the way he closes it up. And I think the one that I skipped there, that's crucial for bringing this dog thing to a, you know, to the end.

Well, it's almost the same date as that which was Mariner and it's a . . . I mean it's more overtly on the subject. It's called:

THE DELINEATION

No longer the unmarked features
require sympathy or any such pity
forlorn compromise with death-dealing
murder the Lybian night-mare put out
to pasture her many-folds of tresses
swaying no longer the stale smoke-
filled rooms but salubrious breezes
she controls as ever the waves over
which nothing rolls unheeded the
steeds return to their places in
the loins where the courses of the
stars keep like Orion trying to tell

us something the way they plow the
sky and how the lines of being show
up in the face of the beloved Amazon

I was going to say amazing Amazon but it gets through, it feels like
that. Remember Wonder Woman?[35] She's too old. So that's a run
through. Like clusters of grapes. You got questions? Was it like the '60's
rehearsed?

The only way, I mean I think that's only in this sense possible through
inflection. And we got the touch and it might be susceptible to a mani-
fold of inflective impulses, whatever you come at it with. I don't know
what no punctuation really means. This certainly isn't put up as some
. . . anything more than an incompetence. See, you can only use what
. . . remember when he makes a distinction in there between the differ-
ent kinds of belief and this other thing called . . . not pseudo, half-? I
mean there are two kinds of, even, non-belief. And when you make up
something, this would be the distinction between fiction and inven-
tion. If you made up something that wasn't absolute belief in Lawrence's
definition, it wouldn't complete the map. I mean it wouldn't be a . . . it
has to be unknown to her is what I'm saying. 'Cause if it isn't unknown
to her then she already knows it and knows it better than you do. So it's
a matter of knowing where you get it. So that, you know, that is the oral
responsibility of the moment plus . . . plus, you know, the things we've
kind of implicitly accorded to it, you know, speed and some kind of
endurance. I mean it has to be something, like he says, "your gods," so
that it's something the order of . . . what only, not a human being. I'm
speaking specifically men and women, man and woman, but what Ol-
son has on that, that's coming from a human being, that thing on that
map. This is after that, if you can hear Genesis that way, as the thing
that caused the . . . well, like fault, you know.

Well it's invention in the same sense as like when the First Lady says
well, "What are we going to do now?" And he says "China." That's all.
And John Weiners[36] said it two if not three years ago that a . . . but you
know how a poet is supposed to be, a little prospective of his nation
and taking care of it . . . and John is one of the more responsible poets
we have in America. Or the American continent so as to include Fred[37]
and everybody—or Neruda gets the prize, right? He says he can't write
poems now that he's in politics. Imagine that! That's like Williams be-
ing knocked out at the guy Aaron Burr shot, Hamilton?[38] Is that who

Burr shot? He's dying and he says, "Perhaps I was misinformed about the man." He hounded him for thirty years, just did a duel with him in which he got himself killed and then he says, "Perhaps I was misinformed about the man." And Dr. Williams says, "Misinformed!"

I mean how far is this going to go, like he and Ezra agreed it wasn't . . . Lawrence calls it Urdumheit.[39] It wasn't original sin but original stupidity. So for awhile, I mean, he's so burdened with that guilt that the poor Adam . . . it never occurs to him that she's the one who's split and went off to see the man about the apple. And once the thing is kind of in focus, Don Juan says, clarity follows fear, I think. Isn't that right? Isn't that your text? Well, I like the Bible still, you know, because it's Sunday.

All the way up here I listened to those guys, like Armstrong-type guys,[40] not the astronaut but the old whatever his name is, and he even played tapes of his father, played them doing the thing, now he's gone—"see still there." It was great.

It's before in Olson's sense of pre. He did an interview with the Paris Review in which he said that he was there in the Garden, he was, before Eve did that, and he was now, and he was inventing this, like that poor guy who was tried for it, saying "Yeah I was there befo . . ." then he kept remembering "I was th . . . , I was even, I was, I was even there before Ad . . .. I was even there before the Serpent. I was in the Garden. I was the gardener of the Garden. Just me and the Serpent." I mean it was like pre pre pre pre, you know, and then pretty soon you think, "Oh yeah, Genesis has been a burden to our lives." You know, why don't we just say "yeah," and then go ahead. Freud called it a repetition compulsion. It repeats that same triang . . . , it's like the triangularity of life that that first poem is talking about. It ends up like a pyramid. Any initiatory procedure is triangular.

It's like Blake's poems about the poison tree, "I asked a thief to steal me a peach."—that kind of stuff. It's him, this other guy, and the lady. That's what I mean. Any questions? Do you? You know all this stuff?[41]

Not married? Women's Lib?

Sanders calls it "Chauvo"! They were all yelling in the audience night before last. Guys would say, "read the Gobble Gang". He'd say "Chauvo!" What was the other one they wanted? "Read Tilly The Toe Queen," you know. "Chauvo!" Wow, he was marvellous, his last line was something like "I scuffled, I grovelled, I conquered" and he left, and somebody said "What about Attica?" And he said, "Attica who?" He was getting very, very, you know, carnival-like. And that's his subject obviously.

I don't want to get into that really, but he's really found out. Doing this, being this, what he called "Frogman Alert" in the old days, and he's continued, and now he's really done it. Peace Eye is Peace Eye and it really is Private Eye, and it really is peace eye, and if it's specific it's like that third dispensation that, when you're Homer, Dante and Melville, then you have the Pacific and I mean he's right there. Pacific is pacific, you know.

And when I was talking about the conversation the First Lady might have with the President, and he doesn't know, but he says, "China". And what I'm saying is that you gotta be at least consonant with your nation. And I would hope there was more. Robin Blaser is kind of the inventor of this thing called Pacific Nation.[42] Which really was the reason for our having gone to Vancouver and been really interested, really interested in going there because of Robin's inventiveness over these six . . . these years, and especially the '60's.

But what I mean is, I don't think that private man . . . I don't mean human being, I mean a man, not generic . . . a man's responsibility isn't any different if he's also not . . . if the pyramid, if the eye in the pyramid, if that thing is really, like Ed would say, "snuffed". Which I think the experience of the '60's would show and I think it will show up later as having accomplished, then I don't think anyone's situation is any different. You gotta find your China, and I think it is China. It's the same guy, but that's because I've studied Blake since 1957. So that I can hear Albion and Jerusalem in that sense, as animate figures and not as simply international or national designations.

I mean that's only like training in the imagination of what he called "Giant Forms". So that was a particular choice to really get out of a sociology. I mean that was the thing that was in the form of existentialism at that moment when I went to school, that's what the trap was. Or, Lawrence in that great letter says that, they get as far as the crucifixion and then say, "poor us," you know, poor us and, what's he say? "Give us . . . don't give us egotism give us death," Not the death of egotism but "the death of a man" right? That would stop there at seven. Like, say, stop at the assassination, which doesn't give you what happened instantly after the assassination, which in the new introduction to Leary's prison memoirs that Ginsberg introduced,[43] he says that what

Leary found was that the men inside did have a pinup, like an image of a woman who was it? Incredibly, I mean, he wouldn't believe it either, Jackie![44] But what was the image of Jackie? Can you imagine what it was? I mean how close after the assassination? She's leaving him, she's crawling out over the trunk. You remember that picture? That was the one they had up as where it was at.

They all had different interpretations, but it was just that pure image of her on the trunk going the other way before that secret service guy helped her back in. And so there's a lot of speculation as to what she was doing, but the point was that she was doing that. I don't know exactly how I got to prison, Attica. What was it that triggered that?

Audience: What I want to know is what's going to happen in the '70's, just in those terms?

Well that's generally what the question really is. The normal man's responsibility being no different from the President's—and he called it "China". Robert Duncan once said that the reason Blake did his final great prophecies was because he had found his Newton. He had his Newton. And we've been on, in spite of Blake's work we've been on and still on. That's another thing, that's in Ginsberg's introduction of Leary's book, as to how long we've been on the Newtonian cosmology. You know there've been lots of them after and before, but we still somehow assent to that without, maybe . . . 'cause Van Gogh said "Life is round." Maybe because of some kind of repetition or circularity that we prefer to the triangle, which I think must be it, don't you think? Don Juan said the true shape of a human was round, which isn't weird. Plato says that. And that's the beginning of his time. And some guy, you know, they got cut like an egg with a hair. So that's the imaginative experience of it. But I think it's being able to, to invent the thing or find the thing.

It's one area at this moment, not Newton but "China" 'cause you must invent, not the, not the language. That was another interesting thing that Sanders said.[45] The reason he could crack the case was because it was a system of language. That's how he finally did it: by seeing it was a language all the participants in the thing spoke and understood. There was a coherent . . . like architects talk of the vocabulary of this place, that's part of the vocabulary. And he was using it as an analogy with how a man can possibly learn the unknown, the unknown unknown.

That's how to study something that's forever unknown. To trust something.

Audience: Isn't the idea? To step out of the circle?

I think not go into it.

Audience: But if that's the condition of man as given, he's in it to begin with.

No, that's the condition of angel before he was cut. Like that last thing, the sickle poem, before he was . . . before Cronos castrated Uranos. They use that same sickle when Ullikummi is defeated.[46] It's the same sickle. Go down and get that one, they tell him. Same one that Heaven and Earth were parted by in the first place. Or, it's like the advice "Honour your mother and your father," Jesus put it. Don't get hung up that way. You still have to say "Woman, what have I to do with thee?" But at the same time you don't say "Ahhh, my old man's a drag."

And you have to invent that, that's all 'cause nobody is going to give you anything to go on. It literally has to be invented. So that finding your Newton or finding your China policy is, is your foreign policy. It's like finding your foreign policy so you can address the unknown. China is the unknown. It's like they call it inscrutable and all that but really it is. You have to think of it as dimensionally different, that the old East and West meeting is not any, you know, Kipling triteness.

I feel that the dog stuff is coming in right on it now, on the wing of it. That image of the unknown unknown. If you ran it, although it'd be a long run, you'd find that China was cognate with what Thompson called The Hound of Heaven.[47] Did you ever hear of that long piece of poetry?

A lot of this material will be presented in the final Maximus poems. That will be what, about eighteen months, two years? So you see what kind of a timetable we're on for that.

I stopped at a gas station on the way in and it said, DON'T ASK US ANYTHING. IF WE KNEW ANYTHING WE WOULDN'T BE HERE. And that's exactly the point. We are here but we don't know anything. But you're being asked. And they're saying, don't ask us anything 'cause if we knew we wouldn't be here—that says it perfectly. We are here, we don't know, but we're being asked and you can't say don't ask because the time has come, and she's saying "Where do you come from?" And if marriage is further than death, well what are you going to say?

You've got to say where you come from. Since you don't know and it's not science fiction, you can't say "I come from Mars." You have to invent the actual ground of your being. Just like that guy did when it came right down to it and he confessed until there wasn't any more, until he had the competency to go out and do it, what they had charged him with.

And a society—America is that woman, and in the middle Maximus poems she is the Lady of Good Voyage. She is there. I don't know what the whole new thing will look like but . . . .

Canton, New York
December 12, 1971

APPENDIX A

THE DOOM OF THE PEARL

fill the room with sperm let it
fill all mouths all eyes all ears
orifices holes in the wall where
pictures once were cracks in the
plaster so the leak in the ceiling
is no longer a problem the floor
a swirl of gaping bodies producing
& receiving their delights so sin
may rebegin the instant you stop
short of giving all look out see
stars catch one place it in the
nave of the Beloved or the Mouse
will ['broken off]

Oxford 12-16-70

NOTES

[1] *North Country Medicine*, edited and published by Al Glover at Canton, New York. "That letter" refers to a December 19, 1914 letter by D. H. Lawrence published as the Christmas, 1971, issue of *North Country Medicine*.

[2] Dr. Clarke's reading was given in Griffith's Art Center, room 123, at St. Lawrence University, Canton, New York.

[3] D. H. Lawrence, *Studies in Classic American Literature*, 1923.

[4] At the time of the reading (and still to my knowledge) Al Glover scouted the country for what he could bring home to measure, giving the truth to Dr. Clarke's term, house organ.

[5] John Clarke, "A Mole to Join Gloucester to the Nation", *Fathar* 4. The title was taken from Charles Olson's poem called "Melkarth of Tyre".

[6] The number of the room in Griffith's Art Center was 123.

[7] *Portents* 19, published by Samuel Charters in an edition of 100. 14 1/2 x 18 inches. Large black and white photo of Olson standing on a pier in Gloucester in his corduroy jacket, before his hair was long, but with stubbly beard and glasses, looking down at an amulet he fingers in both hands. In the sky, to his left, is printed in small type:

> When there were no depths
> I was born, when there were no sources
> of the fountains of the sea
> (sd Maximus) . . .
> At hands length I now grapple
> to confine
> the overlapping flaking
> of the corn, no waves
> I am left with the fine edge
> of my amulet fingered
> in my pocket, if I shaved
> any longer I'd try
> the neolithic razor
> on my hair, the sea

is postcard

of my fountain
(he continued)

[8] The new Maximus poems, under the direction of Dr. George Butterick, [had] not yet appeared.

[9] Charles Olson, *Maximus IV, V, VI*, Cape Goliard, 1968.

[10] *Fathar*, edited by Duncan McNaughton from Buffalo, New York, then moved to Bolinas, California. *Fathar* has done six issues to date, of which number III was devoted solely to the work of John Clarke.

[11] *Magazine of Further Studies*, published six issues from Buffalo, under the editorship of John Clarke, George Butterick, Al Glover and Fred Wah. #6 has extracts from Lawrence's poem "New Heaven & Earth".

[12] Ohio being the mid-west. John Clarke was born in Bellevue, moved to Port Clinton, then Bowling Green.

[13] D.H. Lawrence, *Studies in Classic American Literature*, 1923—"The goal is to know how not-to-know."

[14] John Thorpe.

[15] The text for the extracts of D.H. Lawrence's *Studies in Classic American Literature* used here and elsewhere in this book are from the Penguin edition, 1971, and full acknowledgements are given here to the copyright.

[16] *The Vinland Map and The Tartar Relation*, Yale University Press, 1965. See also *Brittannia*, edited by Daniel Zimmerman, Buffalo, 1970.

[17] Al Glover.

[18] The Institute of Further Studies met at Simon Fraser University, Burnaby, British Columbia, November 10-13, 1970. Professors Ralph Maud and Robin Blaser did all of the ground work and assumed the burden when the Canada Council abdicated on political grounds. George Butterick's talk was listed as "Charles Olson: the Entailment". Albert Glover came in on "The Crow of Odin," Fred Wah addressed "The Poets Who Are Here," and John Clarke presented "The Present Thrust of Further Studies." According to some it was this meeting that produced what changes have taken place in west coast writing recently.

[19] *Magazine of Further Studies* #6.

[20] Lohengrin, see Otto Rank, *The Myth of the Birth of the Hero*, 1932.

[21] Charles Olson, "The Animate Versus the Mechanical, and Thought," *Io* #6, Summer, 1969.

[22] nomoi, see Eric Havelock, *Preface to Plato*.

[23] "the tribe," the Zuni of New Mexico. See M.C. Stevenson, *The Zuni Indians*, 23rd Annual Report of the Bureau of American Ethnology, 1905.

[24] Levi-Strauss, *Structural Anthropology*, 1963.

[25] "that book," D.H. Lawrence, *Studies In Classic American Literature*, 1923.

[26] John Steinbeck, *The Pearl*, first published in *Woman's Home Companion*, December, 1945, under the title "The Pearl of the World."

[27] Dr. Clarke refers here to his proposal to give a reading of certain of the poems published in *Fathar* III.

[28] Lewis MacAdams read in the same room Dr. Clarke was reading in, the year before.

[29] The original text of this poem, as published in *Fathar* III, read "maybe I can".

[30] Janis Joplin, now deceased.

[31] Wynton Kelly, now deceased.

[32] Heinrich Zimmer, *The King and the Corpse*, 1948.

[33] John Layard, *Stone Men of Malekula*, 1942.

[34] See Illustrations of the *BOOK of Job*. Invented & Engraved by William Blake, 1825.

[35] A comic book Amazon of the '40's, still alive for some followers of the golden thread.

[36] The poet John Weiners had decided to visit Red China, but was not given the opportunity.

[37] Canadian poet and one of the four founding members of the Institute of Further Studies.

[38] William Carlos Williams, *In The American Grain*, 1925.

[39] "Urdumheit", D.H. Lawrence, *Apocalypse*.

[40] Garner Ted Armstrong, religionist extrordinaire. One can tune him in nights on most attempts at serious air-wave browsing.

[41] Dr. Clarke begins to address the audience here.

[42] Robin Blaser was a professor at Simon Fraser University, author of several books of poetry, and the editor of *Pacific Nation*. His ability to appreciate the universal in poetry is Legend.

[43] Timothy Leary, *Jail Notes*, 1972.

[44] Jacqueline Bouvier.

[45] Ed Sanders, *The Family*, 1971.

[46] Hans Guterbock, *The Song of Ullikumi*.

[47] Francis Thompson, *The Hound of Heaven*, 1890.

I Too Resembled Health

for an American Woman

& so I kept on trying
which was the thing
that Lawrence had said
was the thing to be done
but It was all based upon
the Death of Europe Instead
so I now know America
is brung up on death.

3.28.75

The Web of the Real—Notes on Form

So it took something like NINE MONTHS of a GREAT Year or some such turn of to regain our morphogenetic balance (homeo-stasis)—purity, pure lines, as against homogenization, hybridization, bifurcation, etc., all of which have run out, by birth (chromo-soma), we are chariots of fire (4 Zoas—conversing in visionary forms dramatic, the daily business, the radical of action is form) : the dream of 9 nights ended: all Aquarius: in the condition of our own 'celestial' (given) knowledge (man/angel).

Serpent Orc: with Urizen-Luvah wheeling against the current of creation (rep. comp.) divided-man has been attempting to invent instrumentation to accomplish the impossible (fantasy—to accomplish the prehistoric wish): we never could do it, they could, not us, now only for the first time since, all, initial, fire-flesh electromagnetic. No longer those instruments (of WAR, religion hid in war, Rahab, the grand consolidation, hermaphroditic serpent), of sublimation, the compulsion to repeat the crime. We ourselves—and this is the message, the good news of the resurrection, of the flesh, the word made flesh, that bodies will not die, Eternal Death, they are the medium of translation, there in the middle, between the two, right and left, Eden/Beulah, continually, going forth and returning, watl-hydra!

The Tharmic Western Gate (of the tongue, i.e., the Ear) is open, no longer labyrinth-spiral wandering; the body itself (Tharmas), the covering cherub removed, (t)harmes of the sea, water-deluge, no more fish, DAGON, corn—corruption of: EN-ER-GY, radically, the *term* of being, itself, Karma, Karmas, Kermes, Kerm: All will do what only the Elect could do formerly (or initially the gods; hence a requisite initiation to be initial likewise), like travel with the Sun, tropism, to move other than, nature now reversed: politics replace physics: phusis—

society of events, Eternal events in, intensive. Each person a passage onto himself, the bole of you, the herm-hole-uluu (see Malinowski on Tro . . .)—Inanna-Oannes-Noah, the exceptional ark, no more, not needed, the rainbow covenant fulfilled, chromatic carry: all action momently form. *No symbol of,* sacrifice, sacral—sacred & profane busted professor Eliade et al. Viz The Vision of the Last Judgment, *but pure meaning:* that which exists through itself (Isaiah-Ezekiel on that condition of animation).

Thus the new epistemology: total immersal & total disclosure—in the sense that the acts of mind and perception themselves will display the shape of things (note Goethe's morphology: the phenomena are the Lehre, including yourself—cf. Olson's proprioception). The New Morphology: fire delights in its form. Form is not an *extension* of content, but its radical, action, in the sense of initial organization, consummation, satisfaction, no dancer-dance, no shadow falls between, no spectre, no content to be shaped, molded, Urizenically, demiurgically—all is flow & form initially, the web of the real, land-shape, Time & Space are real beings (the Human form divine): life is form (stick hole planting—method/process): Morphology-Cosmology: the Story of Creation (Genesis & Appolonius of Tyana on the order of things—mythos/logos): correct proceeding—the liberal/numeral: SHAPE, the bounding line, the Form of things.

Hence what happens when: Heaven & Earth are in true dipolar relation once more: Tree; event; trope; you; turn, by affection. Life is Art, Ort-Ord-Order orders itself: begrunden; middle voice takes care of Mac Leslie 1) the Horse Opera for WEST: 2) Sci fiction for SPACE. Won't do, obviously, never was, a working out of, projection, in place of, like all heroes, especially, they who came so much later than, all the superimposition on everything, hung up, caught, possessed by, prehistorically, what we now can say is not: our story anyway: the serpent stuff in here, between ma & the kid against the pa (the 'primal scene' substituting for an imago mundi, shit, no Imagination, all opera: Weak, weak—O how to get Sig through Mr. B, how to say it big so that it's known, a cosmic psychology, like old Novalis wanted, wow, something like the Sphinx image, that showed, like a pantokrator, spins, no hy-phen, just a Giant Form, image-story (narrative), to be made vertical (like figure-landscape, etc already restored since); attend, awake (sleeper in the land of shadows), the counter-reformation council of

Trent, Michelangelo, shit, why not, that large, no Sistine Chapel, starry ciel and tough basement, above and below, pants down, Earthlings, why not, the heavenly tree grows downward, the lights and airs of the datum, from cause, form-cause, prior, primordial, we have been too long after, meta, something, else, Elysium, no, strawberry fields, virgin mothers all, no serpent-corruption, only heavenly fathers, no sons born against, all for both, for mother, for father, for sister, for brother, for all, no primal horde, no Kronos, no Zeus, as king-shit, no Abel-Cain, blacksmiths, Elohim, rebels against Heaven & Earth: the war that began in heaven has ended on earth, has runout: Aphrodite/Mars/Venus, bullshit, there is no, need for salu, slaughter, for ritual dismemberments, for sacrifices of us to them.

I was in that prehistoric mountain Kur Kronos blacksmith shop with Mr. C. & I's not that interesting, I mean all those bolts shooting through your head, like a bovine blast, no, not at all, the point, I mean we put up with their shit long enough, what a hooker, Los himself forging the Urizenic chain in tears, Promethean titan, Orc all wrong, bondage, mental bondage, the tree of mystery in the brain, the hu-man abstract, alright, wow, we've had enough, Blake sure spotted that and pegged it, by prophecy, or like he said, falsehood is prophetic, that's all I'm saying, pay attention, either way 1) Error, like abounds 2) the term of the 4th, or say the Holy Ghost abroad—the 'little ones'—the weak ones—don't slay them, watch how you go, consider, take away the remembrance of sin, be clear, be careful: Care is the carry (character):

OK, the human *har*vest: violets/news/topos/topicality/tope-ope-eye-plenty-Polis-politics—not by blood, Bad Thing, eating, the filthy host, consume all: death & birth: that war arms redundant fix: show—traum broken, that war is no more because Freud-Blake castration complex is broken, old Oedipus & the world parents, the riddle of the Sphinx, or like what Kronos did to Uranus for the same fucking reason: Christ corrected such corruption (dig the American Indians): which was promised: that the seed of Eve would bruise the serpent's head. Generation finally paid off, which is why I say human harvest, or poisoned wheat-corn-born-darkness visible, now no vegetable glass.

Hence, Angelology (tropos in relation to the other 2): peace is pace, but not strictly passive, like they say in media res, the middle ground, where traction occurs—travel, trade, all tropological activities, or rather in the sense that each event now is triadic—containing all three, to yield the fourth: the Cherubic-angelic power—out of the third comes the one as the fourth: 4; 2; 3; 1:   the making permanent or durable because congruent with process (present creation).   TROY: TOWN— the whole world as, lyre, construction, Tartaros foundation relieved by the turning of it all: Across Space & Time: Hail Aquarius coming in: horologically: trust: no rite of passage, that is your life. In the Confucian middle, an axis mundi, birth on earth | heaven: helicity, the Tao, way-wobble, undulatory wave-ripple, all 6000 years contained in the pulsation of an artery, the blink of an eye, the flash of the white lamp, stroboscopic society restores the real to the real: Areal is hopefully Ariel . . . . ANGEL

so uncompounded is their essence pure . . . . in what shapes they choose—Milton PL

    Color/Heat/Rainbow   *   Sound/Vibration/Lyre

The Blake Sonnets of December 12, 1972

For Jonathan

Unorganiz'd Innocence—An Impossibility

Concerning The Fall of Man—it never happened,
it was an illusion. Man is Eternal, an Eternal
Angel. Every harlot was a virgin once, nor canst
thou ever change Kate into Nan. That is, perfect,
the trick of the ancient Elf. We can think we are
improving our lot, or the human lot, by various
Druidic pursuits, but in assimilating this dissimulation
we like Luvah, are attempting the impossible, which is,
to become more than man. First we are led to believe a lie,
that we are in a fallen State, & then we try to get out of it,
by extending ourselves beyond these limitations, which then become
chains of the mind, which don't exist, are self-imposed,
we, like Albion, are in fact asleep, & in our sleep
all this was created. What can be created can be destroyed.

THE LOST TRAVELLER'S DREAM UNDER THE HILL

Blake is absolutely right, my famous KlogD formula
is only true for Beulah, to aid sleepers in their dreams.
In Eden or Eternity there are no marriages nor are they
given in marriage. Because, equally, sexual division
is of The Fall, Adam & Eve, prior and already before
The Serpent Orc's coming, Reason, the faculty which thinks
it's getting somewhere by practicing the contraries,
the progression from Innocence to Experience. But in
Beulah all contraries are equally true, and we know
what we do has nothing whatever to do with Eden,
where embraces are comingling, & not a pompous high
priest entering a secret place, or hole, or any other
image somewhat of Earth, whatever, it is still
the Son of Morn in weary Night's decline.

The Sleep of Ulro

That is, if you perform your KlogD well in Generation,
since you, like the Lamb, like anything is, apparently,
slain on the stems of Generation, divided continually,
by Acts of Kindness—every kindness to another is a little death
in the Divine Vision—you will get Beulah, or the place
of The Waterers where entropy is reversed, where Emanations
bring you their 'maidens', a little moony world in miniature,
the semblance of Eternity, but still, basically, Threefold,
& if you try to seize its 'inmost form', that is, try to
make it Eden it will shatter, for all was turned
to Samsara by that evil in the garden, and so you
return to the Sleep of Ulro, or Eternal Death, which is
what happens to anyone who tries to live their dream,
they go from 2 to 3 to 1, never realizing it was 4 all along.

THE COVERING CHERUB

The Covering Cherub, with his flaming sword revolving
every which way is image of impossibility of re-entering
Paradise, the place where we already really are.
It is the attempt to do just that, that is, go down to,
or reduce to, Ulro, myself, alone, my Druid Spectre
armed in gold, to take that on, or reclaim as ally,
the fearful thing I am when after something, even myself,
and see that you are this Covering Cherub, you are
this ever-turning wheel or sword or swastika or
whatever else images perversely the Human Fourfold
strictly as an individuation (or flying saucer) without
the redeeming fact that it is all done *for* someone,
in Milton's case, the six-fold Ololon, to go down
himself to annihilate, her to redeem, Jerusalem.

GIVING A BODY TO FALSEHOOD

That is, the principle of consolidation of error,
or reduction to ground is important only so that
there will be something to annihilate, some stone
to put into the mouth of The Devouring Ghost,
or into the furnaces of affliction Albion leapt only
to find them fountains of the Living Waters,
and it was not that he produced or caused
this transformation, he simply and discretely gave all
of himself to or for another person, in this case, Jesus,
who had likewise 'died' for him, but only in fun,
to show his 'different face', his steadfastness
of Vision, evidenced by the Prophet Los, or Blake
himself wasn't interested in getting better but giving
what he had, a terrific ego, to us, who profit by his act

WHAT BLAKE DIDN'T DO

So it's not so much what he was, Ugly,
but how he reduced it to a knowable, Strong,
and who he was able to give it to, Beautiful,
for the Form of The Fourth to issue forth, where
and when? That is the question, and the answer
is, as Lawrence said, 'not yet', for it is at
this crucial moment when men and mountains
meet. They enter each others' bosoms, The Brotherhood
of Eden, *through* the meetings, not the sexuality,
of their Emanations, as man with man conversing
in the Eternal verities, what Lawrence wanted
and held out for, like Olson, to the last, what
broke their hearts, Blake somehow, perhaps because
ha had no company in those years (I am hid), didn't.

WHAT BLAKE DID DO

He didn't 'leave off', stop, or 'cease from'
what he called Mental Fight. When the going
got tough, he got going. He went ahead anyway,
further, saw that the very thing he was holding out
for, Eternity itself, because he had foreknowledge
of it, was the very thing that would kill him, keep him
exclusive, bound, an Orc not a Los. His Vision,
his very truth would turn into lie if not acted
upon, if he did not do it, which he resisted,
like anyone (Damn the King), but finally came through,
was willing to contend for the truth, then & there,
in Spiritual Fourfold London. That it is the acting
out, not the holding out, that makes a man
fit companion to another man, becoming a woman.

MEN & MOUNTAINS MEET

So he became a woman, that is, allowed his Emanation
to emanate, out there, where other men really are,
so that they, the best ones, might enter him,
not as violation or rape, but freely, this is
the Jerusalem in every man, who is called liberty
by all the sons of Eden. This is the liberation which
(as gay lib) women's lib is twin to, first
the woman in Beulah, then the man in Eden, continually,
throughout Eternity, the most minute, the Little Ones,
and the very largest, the giant forms conversing
in visionary forms dramatic, too thunderous for weak
emanations hiding inside, in Beulah's moony night,
for the hidden heart is laid open. She who adores not
your frowns will never adore your smiles (Catherine).

NOT BY JOSTLING IN THE STREET

Or as Charles put it, he was the blue diorite stone monster,
Ullikummi (standing on Main St), fucked by Enki, Lord of
Wisdom, that a man must go out at high noon,
not as Gunslinger (irony), but in 'drag', wearing
the blue vestments of the sea, the Lady of the Lake,
not the Long-House or men's fraternal order—no secrecy
in Art—but simply outside. Not old men in youth cult,
not even Dear Odin on The Tree, single, yourself to yourself,
not even The Gold Machine, alchemie, but only Albion,
and in our own case, America, the soft soul of
Ed Sanders saw, Oothoon, outside the circle of
influence, far from the Rules of Sea-Faring, where we
quietly take off our clothes and enter our chariots of
fire, away from all Female Space, sweet science reigns.

PARADISE

For all this begins in Albion's loins, in the place of seed,
from where Luvah and Vala flew up into the head and heart
in the first place, now returning to their proper stations,
so that man may not think himself queer for wanting
other men, an open society, free of restraint & coercion,
a real agora, a City yet a Woman, this is the where,
now the when, when a man, after liberating a woman—
O thankless task (no holiday load)—goes home to his
proper abode, as prophesied, as imaged in the swan song
of Plato, Atlantis, the true Republic (America), only
because there when we, like Gilgamesh, go to it,
when we leave Married Land and cross over the plain
or Great Waters to meet others likewise translated,
as the Eternal Enoch, to Dilmun, or Tula, *gone.*

IN A BOX

Where all the husbands of the wives go (in a box)
when their travelling (mental) is done, when hats
become ears easily, not through endless transformation, but
Eternal Identity, the consequence of Dike and Goodly Themis,
that order does exist, and is revealed when someone
enters his Chariot of Fire, his Covering Cherub, his
own ability to go out (outward), not in search of
(that is women's work), but to bring to give something
back, that he took (the fire, the apple, the cherry),
to put it back on the Tree it came from, to return it,
to its proper place. This is the Third Town, its destruction,
so life, as David says, may live. A going forth and
returning wearied. Not as in The Pleistocene. No
Stone Venus now, not the Mother, but the Daughter.

CATHEDRON

The Virgin, then (Ololon), by going out the door
(of death, Cathedron), but only in the day of
Divine Power, when the will may be bended,
not before, to emerge from The Mundane Shell,
which is woven out of an apron string. When
the moment is ripe, when was it for Blake? Apparently
told in *Milton* after She entered his garden & he saw
how only he might converse with the man Milton.
He becomes a solar hero through union with Los,
his inner-sun, and is able to make the passage of
all sun-downers, through the Gate of Los, freed
from chauvinism, Enitharmon emanates, & it is
presumably in this stance (with Western Gate open)
that he confronts the soldier in The Garden 1803.

The Change

His first act of 'change', to cast out The Serpent
bodily, almost cost him his life. A long-standing
passive manner with his active physiognomy had caused
him much mischief, he said. Wrath, his weakness.
But it was a salutary act, because he found something out,
what he had always known, that it is better to speak out
than dissimulate, even though one knew himself to be in error,
that it was his 'foolish pride' had caused it, finally,
saw it was himself who wanted to leave the garden, & that
poor Kate was practically kicking him out via the soldier-
king-tyrant. It wasn't long after that he 'crossed over'
the Twenty Years of Darkness, that is subdued his Spectre,
thus organizing his innocence to the point where
he could be private in public (return to Public Address).

THE LIGHT

And public in private (atop indulging in abstract follies
at home), he had at last something uniquely his own
to put before public view, something non-domestic,
non-analytic, non-dark. By light, the Light of Youth,
he told his friend it was he had at last recovered, that is,
his femininity, he had *become black* or Blake his 'dark-
eyed', black-haired maid, so could now give light (and
no longer attempt to change Kate into Nan, or Himself
into his opposite). He was Eternally Light, & his horses
were Urizen's from the beginning, he had simply been a Luvah
in bondage to his Dark Lady, or rather had stolen her from
his 'Good Angel', a redundance and an irony, as one now sees.
Only Love, not Reason, is the way, for our offerings are
rejected yet true friendships prevail, and succeed.

THE INTERPRETER

He gave us the daughter, Jerusalem, we are to become,
not wives (Britannia is Albion's wife), not His
Emanation, a Society yet a Woman. He left
the Lesser Mystery (Beulah) for us & went on
to confer the Greater, so that it would be there
whenever we got to it, whenever we were ready to go
out across all space & time each day as we go to work
or whatever little seeds of light she has gathered for us
to plant, out there in the midst of things, here where men
contend for truth and get tired, overthrown, anything
but discouraged, for your example of disciplined life
shows the way, all the way, though we may, at times,
like you, get mixed up and think such discipline can
turn us into the thing we want, happily not possible.

THE BLAKE AGE

Somebody again takes the initiative in conversation
and I let him because I don't know anything
but that he's like me, and we'll switch back
and forth, not puzzling or figuring over each other
but giving each other the benefit of the doubt, and
speaking plainly about Fatherly concerns, not as to why
this or that thing is but allowing that such things do exist,
though tenuously, and must be brought up carefully and with
brotherly love, for there is no other Eden and Land of Life
than that which exists through itself, imagined by members
of one's own species., when in the profound act of projection
what is hidden to corporeal understanding feels nonetheless
fully organized and solid, as a man must feel when he has given
voice to something heard by another as the interpretation he trusts.

TOWARD A #6

EDITED BY ALBERT GLOVER

Riding the Bull Home

Mounting the bull, slowly I return homeward.
The voice of my flute intones through the evening.
Measuring with hand-beats the pulsating harmony, I direct the endless rhythm.
Whoever hears this melody will join me.

*The only transitive action that is
conceivable and effective is that
of helping each man to encounter
his Imam*

This book dedicated to Henry Corbin

By Friday night got to

  'These Images' of Mr. Yeats

    & find that it *is image*

    & that image *is rhyme.*

P.S.

  & Yes, of course,

death is West

Note that Gawain refuses the Ring but takes
the small green girdle, a mere bit of lace,
that she was wearing about her waist.

"Sir Gawain, by refusing to become the lord
consort of the dazzlingly beautiful shadow-
queen, withstands the temptations that would
transform him into a fairy-bound, divine,
everlasting spectre. By not capitulating to
the generative principle of the life that is
bound with death, the hero disengages him-
self from the self-consuming cycle . . ."

Al'

There are certainly several ways of looking at it, but at this point *the point* would seem to be to (simply) get out of the way.

> "that the world of things isn't the block the lyric throws
> in the way of nature; and Hesiod's *epistamenos* to describe
> the manner of his own composition, belongs to us (as well as
> that Sophia of his, & of Celtic and Norse and Vedic poets
> and Arthurian English tale-tellers"
>
> (Charles Olson,
> "A Comprehension"

So that the noose or net of Herakles of your G.R.S. (*the* Quest) Mead is more proper cover—"the knot, the knot"—than any other variant I–E guys, even Zeus with juice, for trouble is still

> *NO* individual ought to appropriate to
> himself any of the Universal Characteristics

That is, (only) *The Years As Catches* [Cf. H.D. 5 "Occult Matters," last line:

> "But in my life dream, I have not
> seen the Maiden, for I stand in
> her place or in her way."

CORBIN calls it the error of assimilation (*tashbih*) of the dissimulation (*talbis*)

> [what Creeley is getting at in his Day Book, the
> attributes of Subject, from some other French
> phenomenologist]

---- or the Slinger's gun pointed at Infinity ----

        (as, Dear Fred, knew all along:

              to reverse Speculative

          & Applied

                  WINTER APPLES &

                      MIRROR

    position

      "Jabir can become (or rather, becomes) the *Hujjat*,
     the mirror in which is revealed (mazhar) the Imam"
     (Corbin)

So it is the Veil itself that reveals –
not quite,

        "the mirror is the 'place' where the Image
         shows itself but is not its substrate"
         (Corbin)

   pure category (half-moon beach! mirage

        LYRICK BLOCK OUT
        EARTH VORTEX PASSED
               (John's 'Woe')

    "Thereupon the Angel Gabriel makes himself
    visible, proclaiming: 'I am the sixth of you
    five' (*ana sadisukum*), which means the distinct
    personal unity that is also their totality."   (Corbin)

this is the *VALA* problem Blake wrestled with
almost all his life, until Felpham, when Virgin
Ololon arrives in his garden

[see *Milton*]

The Mantle of Years

I plucked Leutha's flower
And I rose up from the vale;
But the terrible thunders tore
My virgin mantle in twain.

(*VDA*
Lambeth 1793

Nor cans't thou ever change Kate into Nan.

I also was surprised to find
the key people at both Vancouver
& San Francisco more receptive to
the IFS than to C.O. whom they
are afraid of or are—they think –
misunderstood by. Likewise when
both Creeley & John were out there
they blew the lid off that lazy society
they have or have arrayed for them-
selves as a kind of last stand

       to preserve that remnant of sanity –
they think—left over from the
last squeeze or push of the 50's

       so were greatly offended by any
direct challenge, as I say by the poets
but rather susceptible

to being treated as Sheave III –
those who live in doubts & fears
perpetually tormented by the Elect

       and really grasping at the chance
to drop their guard & simply cry out
their desperation & plight

       they have— the older ones –

       great beauty & dignity

What do you think of the
idea of Institute matches?
With visual concentration piece
plus inner texts to be read.
Everytime the urge to light
up hits—or a 'song' to be
sung / oral-oral atl-atl.

This is the closest I can
come to a portable cheap
everyday carry-on-you
give-away bull-roarer
or such other *simple*
inventions of past circles
of friends. Quick exchanges.
        innocuous, charming,
fun, harmless –
at the same time full of
power & use for those
who want, or care to strike,
        like, got a light, buddy?

For my Pat

If it were   true
what the Theosophists say
who would ever
        put a match out

That is, conceivably, another chance at pure religious category—along

with the current retaking of story, ritual, etc. - e.g. the dogma of
ORIGINAL SIN (so weakened by Mr. Pelagius that at our end "GOD
IS DEAD") and *theology* as a science, what was so noticeably missing
from 2001, like OUT of it, there

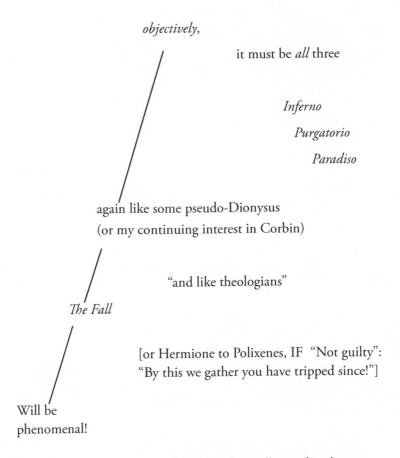

objectively,

it must be *all* three

Inferno

Purgatorio

Paradiso

again like some pseudo-Dionysus
(or my continuing interest in Corbin)

"and like theologians"

The Fall

[or Hermione to Polixenes, IF "Not guilty":
"By this we gather you have tripped since!"]

Will be
phenomenal!

but since, but still—*nothing* but
the End of the Christian Religion

P.S.

>   – Could we *invent* pure machines?
>
>   (out of the airs & lights
>
>   of the datum ? ?)
>
>   of knowing?

A physics, or physical vocabulary

– of 'phi-units'   <u>WORDS</u>

      to construct

    (like the *Gates of Paradise*):

      Keys to the Kingdom

   Or simply then to be able to *See* the forms

of the present & the *trans*-forms

they are : so that the whole thing

ceases simply to be topological?

Radically ,

    what is the nature of passwords?

Returning from supper I think I see now more clearly His golden food

The Pangs of Eternal Birth are better than the Pangs of Eternal Death

                    Let even your mother

            go. Let there be only paradise

                                        to be out of hell

                    know what wind / lifts it away

                                        The Vent!

. . . #6 not death—death is next #7—actually annihilation—so six is (like sex is) what you say it is: CLEARWATER REVIVAL—that's it, the quote *other* geography—mental landscape—suprasensory topographies—inside our turbans—the slow westward movement – HOME—homeward bound—or the getting there by paths that have heart (don't look back)—the adherence *to*

the orientation of space in time or time x space—in other words, the *rhythm* (don't fall off) method

PERCEPTION: Oedipus' Eyes—the transpersonal moth & fath: the OP issue—*ta'wil*, leading back by going right onward—West to East, literally the discovery of America (& the accomplishment of the sexual revolution); in fact, could use the Lawrence right here

NEW HEAVEN & EARTH
the line would be:
"A fine wind is blowing the new direction of Time"

That is (as he says) "The rock will split, we shall come at the wonder, we shall find the Hesperides

or coming right out of #5. the earth is vortex passed by the traveller, the way to—The Gate of the Tongue, the Western Gate—to where the "apples" are—Avaloa—or the Jung Indian River Map Blake calls Thames Tharmas like Nile Osiris or Orontes-type continuation of celestial river OKEANOS rages to tear love loose (lucymelos—the lucid melody—Cf. Aaron's Rod) that is, the sense of touch

On what is Varuna (heaven) based?
On water.
On what is water based?
On semen.
On what is semen based?
On the heart.

Tharmas, the heart,
(parent power dark-
ening in the West

Paths that have heart (Cf. the Arts called
Gothonic)

Heyerdahl departure next wk—papyrus (Byblos) boat, from Gates of Herakles AFRICA, the heart shaped continent, to Amerika via atl-atl

& any others who are like,
Look Homeward,
Angel . . .

Yes, as you say, 'without fear'
& to the extents that this is
misunderstood [I learn the status
of Kali—*the divine mother of the
universe*—in the Indian Room
of the British Museum is labelled

"Kali—Destroying Demon"]

humanism (The British Empire) remains
rampant still or should I say *blatant*, the last
cries, 'the MOB'—what Spenser
saw almost from the beginning

THE BLATANT BEAST

or why terror succeeds –
it's good for business. (like heresy itself)

——————————

Kafka & the others got as far
as "the Bug"
but that is still a 'SLAVE MORALITY'
such as Nietzsche noted is based on
the 'ressentiment' of those denied the Real
re-action, the DEAD, who compensate
by ('imaginary') *revenge*: thus requiring
a Counter-World, or like simply
to have a counter, counter
to be on one side or the other of

——————————

(But since the Beatles have gone for the Apple,
and given that up too—as you know—the
MOB literally scarfed it up, building
and all—total renovation;
I think what's in store is more in store
in *what* you SEE
today happening:

Nature is a Vision of the Science of the Elohim   at the moment
                    I'm, I don't know

Vainamoinen old and wily greeted
the little copper man
emerging from the waves
with the strange words— –

          'most contemptible of men, no
          better than a dead man are you
          with a face like a corpse'

—— he evidently alluding to the newcomer's kinship
with the souls of the dead! Those whom you must now needs know,

          old-bearded-snake-youth-Themis-cup-grail-knight-life-like-
          last-supper-banquet-blood-wine-bath-amber-Daimon-Dionysos-
          Agathos-death-down-dawn-drawn-cave-grave-gate-*go*

greet Osiris in Sacer Ludens? No sacrifice. No offering. No gifts
to the dead. Child of the Cretans fed
by a swarm of bees (who were souls!) had
something of that smell of the dead about him,
his cave had that property they said also
who had been to Mount Lykaion. . . .
                    /
                         The terrors of Tantrism only
               (& possibly that other Armenian Shylock knew)
          the meaning of
                         Fish, flesh, fowl
                    not any season-séance long -----
only this jealous burning up
the stake-stalk of ourselves
               mounted backward in our time,
               the many-colored raiment
               'emanating'

Here's one for the kid when he, like, grows up
to find *a reality equivalent to his own*
come into being

> "Myson, the misanthropist, was once surprised
> by one of those people as he was laughing to himself.
> 'Why do you laugh?' he asked; 'there is no one with you.'
> 'That is just why I am laughing.' said Myson."

> from Schopenhauer's
> *Studies in Pessimism* –
> underscored by Melville
> Rimbaud Wieners Olson &
> now yr father . . .
> in his time

> O be mine,

St. Valentine's Day, 1969

No — #6 is not marriage   See the other Zimmer, *King & the Corpse*
      story of Sir Gawain   until 'death' — which is #7 —
                       is accomplished (the meeting with the
                                        Green Knight)

#8 Marriage — the polity & stratagems of married love —
is not possible

          You'll notice the knight gets a scarf or girdle
       or *veil*,
             like the Mantle Leucothea gives Odysseus
             (Bk. V)

             (& by the way, Leucothea when she was Ino,
           an earthling girl, Kadmos's daughter,
               was the mother of Melicertes, that is,
               HERAKLES

      In other words, a White etc. Goddess, like Blake's
      Vala, a mother-wife-sister-consort, *Luvah* the 'dying' god

Whereas, the marriage following (heiros gamos) — the polity of love —
is between Albion & Jerusalem (he the eighth, as *Jesus* the seventh)

                  Eye

                  OP   plenty
                            apples
                            Fred
                            was talking
                            about not
                            passing out
                            until . . .

BIBLIOGRAPHY

I. BEGINNING

a. Actions & gestures

Human Origins: Selected Readings. University of Chicago, 1946.

Jung, C.G. *Psychology and Alchemy.* Pantheon Books, 1953.

Olson, Charles. "Notes on Language and Theatre," *Human Universe and Other Essays*, San Francisco: The Auerhahn Society, 1965.

Osborn, Henry Fairfield. *Men of the Old Stone Age.* Charles Scribner's Sons, 1918.

b. Continuance

Hawkes, Christopher. *The Prehistoric Foundations of Europe: To the Mycenean Age*, Methuen, 1940

Hyams, Edward. *Dionysus: A Social History of the Wine Vine.* Macmillan, 1965.

Mellaart, James. "Anatolia Before c. 4000 B.C.," and "Anatolia c. 2300-1750 B.C.,

– *Cambridge Ancient History*, Fascicle #20.

– "Anatolia c. 4000-2300 B.C.," *Cambridge Ancient History*, Fascicle #8.

– *Catal Huyuk: A Neolithic Town in Anatolia.* McGraw-Hill, 1968.

– "The Earliest Settlement in Western Asia: From the Ninth to the End of the Fifth Millennium B.C.," *Cambridge Ancient History*, Fascicle #59.

Wooley, C.L. *The Sumerians*. Norton, 1965 (pp. 5-9, citing Sir Arthur Keith, *Al-'Ubaid*).

Esin, U., and P. Benedict. "Recent Developments in the Prehistory of Anatolia," *Current Anthropology*, vol.4 (1963), 217-39.

Hood, M.S.F. "The Tartaria Tablets," *Antiquity*, XLI (1967), 99-113.

Piggott, Stuart. "The Beginnings of Wheeled Transport," Scientific American, vol. 219 (July, 1968), 82-90.

Pope, Maurice. "The Origins of Writing in the Near East," *Antiquity*, XL (1966), 17-23.

Renfrew, C., and J.E. Dixon and J.R. Cann. "Obsidian and Early Cultural Contact in the Near East," *Proceedings of the Prehistoric Society for 1966*, New Series, vol. 32, no. 2, 30-72.

Solecki, R.S. "Prehistory in Shanidar Valley, North Iraq," *Science*, no. 18 (1963), 179 ff.

Clark, Grahame, and Stuart Piggott. *Prehistoric Societies*, Knopf, 1965.

Garrod, Dorothy, and Grahame Clark. "Primitive Man in Egypt, Western Asia and Europe," *Cambridge Ancient History*, Fascicle #30.

– "The Near East as a Gateway of Prehistoric Migration," in G.G. Mac-Curdy (ed.), *Early Man*, 1937.

Howell, F.C. "Upper Pleistocene Stratigraphy and Early Man in the Levant," *Proceedings of the American Philosophical Society*, vol. 103 (1959), 1-65.

– ed. "Early Man and Pleistocene Stratigraphy in the Circum-Mediterranean Regions," *Quaternaria*, vol. 6 (1962).

Jackson, J.W. *Shells as Evidence of the Migration of Early Culture*, Manchester, 1917.

Movius, H.L., Jr. "The Proto-Magdalenian of the Abri Pataud, Les Eyzies (Dordogne)," *Fifth International Congress for Pre- and Proto-History*, Hamburg, 1958 (1961), 561-66.

"Radiocarbon Dates and Upper Paleolithic Archaeology in Central and Western Europe," *Current Anthropology*, vol. 1 (1960), 355-91.

Stone, J.F.S., and L.C. Thomas, "The Use and Distribution of Faience in the Ancient East and Prehistoric Europe," *Proceedings of the Prehistoric Society* vol. 22 (1956), 37-85.

c. Civilization creators

Frankfort, Henri. *Kingship and the Gods: A Study of Ancient Near Eastern Religions as the Integration of Society and Nature.* Cambridge University, 1948.

Kramer, Samuel Noah. "Inanna's Descent to the Nether World," in Sumerian Mythology, *American Philosophical Society, 1944.*

Olson, Charles. "The Gate and the Center." *Human Universe,* 17-23

Pritchard, James ed. *The Ancient Near East.* Princeton University, 1958.

II. EPISTEMOLOGY

a. Substantive

Frobenius, Leo, and Douglas C Fox. *African Genesis.* Faber & Faber, 1938.

— *Prehistoric Rock Pictures in Europe and Africa.* New York Museum of Arts, 1937.

Rank, Otto. *Art and Artist.* Knopf, 1932.

Raphael, Max. *Prehistoric Cave Paintings.* Pantheon Books, 1945.

b. *L'art mobilier*

Hancar, Franz. "The Eurasian Animal Style and the Altai Complex," *Artibus Asiae,* vol. XV (1952), 171-94.

— "Zum Problem der Venusstatuetten im eurasiatischen Jungpalaolithikum," *Praehistorische Zeitschrift,* XXXXXXI (1939-40), 85-156.

c. (Pictures *only*)

Bandi, Breuil, Kirchner, et. al. *The Art of the Stone Age.* Crown, 1961

Breuil, H. *Four Hundred Centuries of Cave Art.* Montignac, Dordogne: Centre d'Etudes et de Documentation Prehistoriques, 1952.

Grand, P. M. *Prehistoric Art.* New York Graphics Society, 1967.

Grasiosi, P. *Palaeolithic Art.* Faber & Faber, 1960.

Kubler, Kooijman, and Movius. *Three Regions of Primitive Art*. New York Museum of Primitive Art, 1961.

Kuhn, Herbert. *The Rock Pictures of Europe*. October House, 1967.

Laming-Emperaire, A. *L'archeölogie préhistorique*, Editions de Seuil, 1963.

Leroi-Gourhan, A. *Treasures of Prehistoric Art*. H.N. Abrams, 1967.

Lommel, A. *Shamanism: The Beginning of Art*. McGraw Hill, 1967.

Maringer, J. and H.G. Bandi. *Art in the Ice Age*. Allen and Unwin, 1953.

Neumann, Erich. *The Great Mother*. Pantheon Books, 1955.

Radin, Paul, ed. *African Folktales and Sculptures*. Pantheon Books, 1966.

Sieveking, A. and G. *The Caves of France and Northern Spain: A Guide*. London, Vista Books, 1962.

d.   (Remains *only*)

Ackerman, Phyllis. "The Dawn of Religions," in V. Ferm (ed.) *Forgotten Religions*. Philisophical Library, 1950.

James, E. O. *Prehistoric Religion: A Study in Prehistoric Archaeology*. Barnes and Noble, 1957.

Levy, G. Rachel. *Religious Conceptions of the Stone Age*. Harper, 1963.

III. History

Sauer, Carl Ortwin. "The Agency of Man on the Earth," W.L. Thomas, Jr. (ed.), *Man's Role in Changing the Face of the Earth*. Chicago, 1956.

"The End of the Ice Age and Its Witnesses," in John Leighly (ed.), *Land and Life: A Selection from the Writings of Carl Ortwin Sauer*. Univ. of California, 1963.

"Environment and Culture during the Last Deglaciation," in *Land and Life*.

"A Geographic Sketch of Early Man in America," in *Land and Life*.

"Seashore-Primitive Home of Man?" in *Land and Life*.

"Time and Place in Ancient America," *Landscape*, vol. 6, no. 2, 8-13.

IV. Mapping

a. Blood

Boyd, William. *Genetics and the Races of Man*. Little Brown, 1955.

Gates, R.R. *Human Ancestry*. Harvard University, 1948.

Smith, M. "Blood Groups of the Ancient Dead." *Science*, vol 131 (1960), 699-702.

b. Ice

Broeker, W.S. "Absolute Dating and the Astronomical Theory of Glaciation," Science, vol. 151 (1966), 299-304.

Ewing, Maurice and William Donn, "A Theory of Ice Ages," *Science*, vol.123 (1956), 1061-66; vol. 127 (1958), 1159-62; vol. 129 (1959), 464-5.

Wright, H.E. Jr. "Late Pleistocene Climate of Europe: A Review," *Bulletin of the Geological Society of America*, vol. 72 (1961), 933-84.

V. Technology

Hawkes, Christopher. *The Prehistoric Foundations of Europe*.

VI. Muse

Cushing, Frank Hamilton. "Zuni Breadstuff," *Indian Notes and Monographs*, vol. VIII, Museum of the American. Haye Foundation, 1920.

Harrison, Jane Ellen. *Themis*. Cambridge University, 1912, 1927.

Jung, C. G., and C. Kerenyi. *Essays on a Science of Mythology*. Pantheon Books, 1949.

Knight, Richard Payne. *A Discourse on the Worship of Priapus*, 1736.

Layard, John. "The Malekulan Journey of the Dead," *Spiritual Disciplines: Papers from the Eranos Yearbooks*. Pantheon Books, 1960.

Malinowski, Bronislaw. *Myth in Primitive Psychology*. London: Psyche Miniatures, General Series, no. 6, 1926.

Melville, Herman. *Moby Dick or, The Whale*, 1851.

Olson, Charles. "Review: *Preface to Plato*, Eric Havelock (Harvard, 1963)," *Niagara Frontier Review*, I (Summer, 1964), 40-44.

Sapir, Edward. *Language*. Harcourt, Brace, 1921.

Snell, Bruno. *The Discovery of the Mind*. Harvard University, 1953.

Sturluson, Snorri. *The Prose Edda*.

Wilhelm, Richard. *The Secret of the Golden Flower*. Routledge & Kegan Paul, 1931.

Whitehead, Alfred North. *Process and Reality*. Macmillan, 1929.

Whorf, Benjamin Lee. *Language, Thought & Reality*. MIT Press, 1956.

Zimmer, Heinrich. "On the Significance of the Indian Tantric Yoga," *Spiritual Discipliones*, pp. 3-58.

VII. Ethics

a. The Earth itself

Frobenius, Leo. *Erlebt Erdteile*, Ergebnisse eines deutschen Forscherlebens. Frankfurt am Main, 1929. In 7 vols.: I. Ausfahrt: Von der Völkerkunde zum Kulturproblem; II. Erschlossene Räume: Das Problem Ozeanien; iii. Vom Schreibtisch zum Aquator; IV. Paideuma: Umrisse einer Kultur—und Seelenlehre; V. Das sterbende Afrika; VI. Monumenta Africana; VII. Monumenta Terrarum.

Humbolt, Alexander von. *Kosmos*. Stuttgart & Tubingen, 1845-1862, 5 vols.

Sauer, Carl Ortwin. "The Morphology of Landscape," in *Land and Life*.

"Terra firma: Orbis novus," in *Hermann von Wissmann--Festschrift*. Tübingen, 1962.

b. & single man

Kirchner, H. "Ein archaelogischer Beitrag zur Urgeschichte des Schamanismus," *Anthropos*, vol. 47 (1952), 244-86.

Narr, Karl. J. "Bärenzeremoniell und Schamanismus in der Alteren Steinzeit Europas," *Saeculum*, vol. X, no. 3 (1959), 233-72.

Vajda, L. "Zur phaseologischen Stellung des Schamanismus." *Ural-altaische Jahrbucher*, vol XXXI (1959), 455-85.

VIII. Politics

a. Megalithic

Chadwick, Nora K. *Celtic Britain*. Thames and Hudson, 1963.

Hallström, Gustaf. *Monumental Art of Northern Europe from the Stone Age*. I. The Norwegian

Localities, 1938; II. Northern Sweden. Stockholm: Bokföriage Aktiebolaget Thule, 1960.

Hawkes, J., and Christopher. *Prehistoric Britain*. Penguin Books, 1944.

Nordman, C. A. "The Megalithic Culture of Northern Europe," in *Finska Fornminnesforengens Tidskrift*, vol. 39 (1935).

Piggot, Stuart. *Ancient Europe from the Beginnings of Agriculture to Classical Antiquity*. Aldine Publishing Co., 1965.

– *British Prehistory*. Oxford University Press, 1949.

– *Prehistoric India*. Penguin Books, 1950.

– "The Tholos Tomb in Iberia," *Antiquity*, vol. XXVII (1953).

Thom, A. *Megalithic Sites in Britain*. Oxford University, 1967.

b. Gothonic

Adams, Brooks. *The New Empire*. Frontier Press, 1967.

Chadwick, John. *The Decipherment of Linear B*. Cambridge University, 1958.

– "The Prehistory of the Greek Language," *Cambridge Ancient History*, Fascicle #15.

Gordon, Cyrus. *Ugarit and Minoan Crete*. Norton, 1966.

Guterbock, Hans. "The Hittite version of the Hurrian Kumarbi

Myths; Oriental Forerunners of Hesiod," *American Journal of Archaeology*, vol. LII (1948), 123-34.

- "Notes on Luwian Studies," *Orientalia*, vol. XXV (1956).

- *The Song of Ullikummi.* American Schools of Oriental Research, 1952; reprinted from the *Journal of Cuneform Studies*, vol. V (1951), 135-61; VI (1952), 8-42.

Harrison, Jane Ellen. *Prolegomena to the Study of Greek Religion.* Cambridge University, 1922.

Hawkes, Sonia Chadwick, H. R. Ellis Davidson, and Christopher Hawkes, "The Finglesham Man," *Antiquity*, vol. XXXIX (1965), 17-32.

Heraclitus, *Fragments.*

Hesiod, *Theogonia.*

Olson, Charles. "A Comprehension," *The Pacific Nation* (February, 1967), 42-44.

- "An Essay on Queen Tiy," *The Wivenhoe Park Review*, II (1967), 37-42.

- "Mayan Letters," in *Selected Writings.* New Directions, 1966.

Sauer, Carl. O. *Northern Mists.* University of California, 1968.

Stubbings, Frank. "The Rise of Mycenean Civilization," *Cambridge Ancient History*, Fascicle #18.

Turville-Petre, E. O. G. *Myth and Religion of the North.* Wiedenfeld and Nicolson, 1964.

Webster, T. B. L. *From Mycenae to Homer.* Norton, 1964.

Vries, Jan de. *Altgermanische Religionageschichte*, 2 vols. Berlin: Walter de Gruyter, 1956.

Note: This bibliography is to be used in conjunction with *Pleistocene Man* by Charles Olson (Fascicle #1 of "A Curriculum for the Study of the Soul," Institute of Further Studies, 1968.)

KNOWLEDGE AND LOVE

for Albert Glover

I

Now we come back
and the Earth
with all its preceding
generations
                    since the two
came apart and caused
a great upheaval
                    which
ever since
            has been
in the way or had to be
cleared
            at great coast
to human life and limb
by those who succeedsd
while Heaven waited
for Eros to loosen.

II

For now
it is all a Vision anyway
anywhere the tree tops
over the tops of the houses
of the city
                    filtering the rays
of the light of the setting sun

& the sounds of
the neighborhood of
dogs & children
playing
    an occasional
adult snatch between
as a jet raises the decibels
overhead
      just as the phone
rings.

III

So when Creeley says
The Plan is the Body
            it must
be taken as
corrected by Lawrence
            to include
both
the man & the woman
The Body of Love
         as the egg
Plato cut to
discover The Mind
          made whole
again as though
it hadn't happened
          the whole
intervening hair of Time.

IV

I will not be
      stuck with
the backside of
Peace
 making   I am

as tough
as the
 next guy   so
refuse entry
on other grounds   than
war until
they come together
                    in Truth
for Real   conversation
                            after
I've made
my point again   to them.

V

The Bowling Green
                    pre-marital
way of seeing
            Things
disconnected
from the mind's
discovery
        of Itself
through 20 years
of darkness
            inside
The Doors of
Perception
            suddenly
remembering the memory
associated with Diz's
playing   came back   here.

VI

The smell of
        Reality
too
        in the air
                of which

Albion begins to
breathe
   The Triangle
vindicated   proving
proposition   Sophia
            never did
sink in
to the matter
        grey matter
reciprocally   I never
drank in
the eyes of   my mother.

VII

So my dear
      Friends
Job
Olson
Hamlet
Brown
  did or do
not   as I
did
     not know
my Ohio Lugal Father
of the Wood
       County Fair
vertu until now—
         gave
up the reins and went
into Real Estate   instead.

            July 10-13 1975

PART II

VIII

The poet now
        will
place himself
        in the hole
of himself
        and come un-
crunched
        before
your very eyes
        to begin
Part II of this work
        ending
Part One begun on
the tenth   concluding
ten days ago
        the ascent from
Chaos.

IX

It is a question
        rather
at this point
        in the Blake
Age—we have come through
the philological & archaeological –

whether one can conserve the social
amenities and still preserve
his stomach
        from the Eaters
of one's own
        Rogo

            still the same
'By double Spectres Self Accurst'
                          if one
allow himself
            the luxury of wit.

X

So like
Rip Van
          Winkle
I wake
up with
          a stiff
neck &
wonder
          if
as I say
one can stay
                here
without going
mad as
          Popeye
almost did:
"Mickey Mantle sucks".

XI

As the word
Herder is
          magical in
itself
nothing else
          he did
is
this
      is what they

don't
know
        yet
but will
when Will
            finally
gets
here.

XII

It is true
one cannot
            hit on
            a person
like I do
the accordion
                working out
my understandable
 aggression
                toward projection –
                inward perfection
by outward   untoward
substitution   inaction
                        means
the anima dies –
                diminishing
the return.

XIII

'A weaker
            sort
survive   and possess
                    the Earth'
'glory is
        humbled'
                with

sufficient energy
                    from
massive hypothetical
vector source
                    to violate
parity
            without becoming
any more
(or less)
            strange.

XIV

The psyche
is risked
in battle
            a battle
is fought for
it   the prize
of battle:
            as long as
my breath remains
in my breast
                    & my
knees
are in motion
                    my
mortality
intact   not to be
tampered with.

XV

One learns   leans
slowly   to break
the Earth Bride's
code

love penetrates
to the heart
    the source of
what is said
    cutting
away the familiar
      contemporary
brambles   the rose
flows   true again
    displaying
the infinite
that was hid
    in dogma.

XVI

Emergence from
the crypt of
    Death
a world   made
of man
& woman   a poem
not alone
    but Kate
included
after Sedition
    made
      Reason's
reclamation
    Life's
necessity
    to stir into being
what had been
caught & taken & hidden.

XVII

No sheep's blood for
                    ghosts
for we are not
in this world for
                    let
but opposition
and progression –
                    nor cancer
spray up
the side of
the building
                by centrifugal force
an Halloween
oranging   of the windows
of the soul –
                    quick
get the
syringe!

XVIII

[But there is
a larger story
                    here
for us
all but
        it
will have
to wait
            for
part Three
            of
this
work
        to

come
out.]

XIX

Which is
        a woman's dying
        or David's
        or a Nation's
breakdown
                fantasies
all
    not real
    blackmail
                so you
feel
    guilt
            instead of
joy
    at wanting
to
play.

XX

So stick
        to your guns
lads, they
revive ten-
            fold!
& if it's real
plan the funeral
                cruel
to be kind
            kith & kin
inheritance
of Fortune

       samsara
blindness   to the Garden
of Delight
       bounded by
the mind's   belief.

XXI

For She, too
        is going
through   the self-same
spell
    if She is
        like Death
real   not ontologically
just   right
       for you   as true
Phantasia
      specifies –

otherwise I will not
urge this
      procedure
      on the future –
men &
women.

Part 3

XXII

Adam & Eve
            & the Snake –
this will be   flawed by
recurrent
creation
            not to mention
the clutter
du text
            nonetheless
methinks it
accordant
            while
I have time
& space to   tell you
                        all
the condition   that We are
in.

XXIII

Doubt
        karma as
        explanation for
anything
            until Figure
            emerge more
into Foreground
                so likewise
                            Background
of history
            as cosmos   as science
fiction
nothing   in fact
                prior to

after you
The Greatest
Story Ever Told.

XXIV

References
        for behavior
        don't ever
            give ground
of
  action—the
  Einsteinian
        Bust is imminent
neighboring powers
          noise   radio-
active   stars
      wheel toys
broken by –
      the Setting Sun
           which
precedes   light
as We   do.

XXV

Paradise is
      obeying something
      more interesting

than anyone can think of
          when
he goes   to sleep
     so
listen   to what
      otherwise
        goes down
& learn

from
Our mistakes
the breaks
for She will
resume Her tending
of the Snake   awake.

XXVI

So it seems
genetic but
it isn't
the Assignment
is as   single as
choice
at any given   moment
time to
wait too –
Measure is Best –
to imagine
how   in the world
you got here
with Us   & why
you're not
satisfied with
Us.

XXVII

Me & Her   that's Us
now
you don't want
to be
The Snake
you're not   even colored
what will
We do

without
     you
        our answer
        Mr Dancer
              is new
We'll die
on you   you'll never know
              what
Love is.   Knowledge is.

XXVIII

For we are back
and you
with all your preceding
information
        since We went
apart and caused
you such travail
        which
even now
     is
in your way   must be
assimilated
       at some price
to your life   & lives
of those you loved
while Knowledge waited
for you to choose   Love.

July 10-23 1975

John Clarke holding up a copy of *The Niagara Frontier Review* at the memorial service for Harvey Brown in Buffalo in 1990.

A Sheaf of Poems 1

THE LAND OF THE BEES

double sonnet for Barbara Cass

Barcelona you remember you were walking
about the room as I was talking to some
others seated around The Round Table on
chairs when suddenly from the far other
end it was like my flat except all open
somehow more like an old Allied Musical
Arts Studio Toledo Ohio but this one is
on the second floor like Harry Martin's
only even bigger anyway the music began
to play and it was Mingus Fingers which
made me swivel instantly to the piano I
Remember Clifford was the tune but only
after some few chords Mingus was saying
Hey Piano Player in that voice that can
strike terror then out of nowhere comes
a guy whose evil face you know from way
back threatening me with "Remember that
barbed wire last night" and then I want
to get out of there but the only way is
by Mingus & the music cause the door is
to the right at their end & then I know
there is no way out & I'm going to have
to face the music & somehow it does not
have anything to do with that White Guy
for you're oblivious to any possibility
of danger and quite comfortable helping
me to do whatever it is in my dream I'm
not doing when I awake to your Dream of

Gloucester
2.28.74

The Sacked Continents of Atlantis & Mu

for Creeley

I
were once established on the main land
then they were driven off but to found
other lands further off than were realized
then the others who had come to realize
that the body was possibly used by same

II
guys who we had all known previously for
their faulty manners or fancy foot-work
across the board we'd thought to proclaim
Here She Comes but She laughing sd/I can't
read your handwriting, My Dear, Oh My.

III
Thought-Earth, what a Creation,
Oh John what do you want to say
I can write you know you can too
so right let's go & She Is There
anyone, go on, smoking TRIUMPH

IV
a beast that once proud discoursed
once had what this record yours will
show, it's called The Lightening Drum,
this is a performance of time, getting
messed up with some water wasn't

V

oracular we just fit the situation
sorry about that, this isn't going to last
if She doesn't come out & prove the body
is the most resistant system in the universe
black is the heart that won't regret

VI

Don't Worry, a tall & honest woman very
black will save you, She really has a cut
on her shoulder, or did before the phone rang
& I can't go on until I hear her snapping
fingers approaching then receding the sound

VII

barrier we all have, Fred, wouldn't you
know She'd circle around & come back &
then to decide My God she is back here
taking something from this very surface
carefully walking off before the line ends.

VIII

Where's it ended? This is a new twist
in itself I wouldn't go any further if I were
you, buddy, let's I mean not get too fucking
automatic I mean if we're gonna do this I
wouldn't the fuck go any further than this.

IX

Sitting here I cannot hold my breath
She just goes on laughing inside of it all &
just stays there, she'd better not knock
anything off important, All Right, moan but
She's putting it all back in place, to touch.

8.22.72
4:51 A.M.

On the Assassination of King Faisal
for Robin

This is just another attempt at this moment
of the world's awakening or striving to become
conscious of itself Fichte said was the point
of history not Hegelian synthesis of opposites
but the dipolarity of King & Republic Novalis
prophesied nothing would last without because
this fiction urges man on to become the Spirit
who in turn becomes the Body not of Fate but
Politic macroanthropically yet almost always
man has confused the leader with the genus
of mankind which could well be the true poet
a geognost not inclined to martyrdom as those
who conspired to kill our kings now complain
of their entrance into the province of power.

3.26.75

JUST THINK WHAT WE WOULD HAVE HAD HAVE BEEN HAD WE HAD THE PROPER AUDIENCE TO DEVOUR THE EXCESS OF OUR DELIGHT

somehow, because of Gerrit, worth it

I trust time, no it's me
when I don't, I say
not you, who lies always
indifferently placed against
the lie of intercourse,

The Woman Who Rode Away,
what a, marvelous unnecessary
tract, how could we have gotten
so far off, it, & put down Alfred
Lord Tennyson to boot for writing

Idylls of the King, & Scott &
Stevenson & all the rest
of them, the 'bad' Authors,
my God, what hypocrisy,
anything that would have

made a difference, should have
been considered, & given
a chance to be heard,
for Our Best otherwise are
stuck with all these problems

to rectify, which takes all their
writing time, out of which could have
come something more primary to
their own location in the world
of things known to them, felt as

such, the many colored raiment
for example, I got from Yeats
as I recall, he too spent most
of his time doing other things,
Ezra's teacher along these lines,

to correct wrong, of fellow men,
and so, Wild Swans At Coole
could remain best achievement,
along with Keats, had he not died
sooner, extending the normal canon

to include such things as don't
really relate to what was really
developing, automatic writing &
everything else we know about
aren't good enough to justify

REVERSE ENTROPY, AFTER DANTE

to Duncan McNaughton

Risk it all, always
come on, heart, put it
back into The System

the only way to
escape being The King
of Death, so much

depends upon
a red wheel barrow,
the Soul itself

under Image of
The Queen of Death
out of Hell at last

the Hainwele Narrative
Atlantean inheritance
lost to memory in

Megalithic Religion
an endless labyrinth
of woe, The Maro Dance

the return to normal,
no muse, no myth, no
allegory, but fable

which is Vision itself
because, like gravity,
it can't be bent, or

deflected, there is
no break, it is all,
in the continuity of

life itself, if you can
give it up, put it in,
let it go, what it was

was your own, desire
to be loved, completely,
without action, passion,

sacrifice of something,
without substitution
you find it's you, all

along, continuous
annihilation, actually
the Human in question

miraculously survives
as in The Rose Garden
of fabulous Apuleius

had a sense of humor
so made him naked in
front of everybody,

who couldn't care less
whether you do this
or not, it's just done,

twenty years of being
an ass is enough, ten
ought to do it nowadays,

at the end of Pisces
we have lots of vesture,
the many-colored raiment

Yeats predicted with
his gyres & things, so
we wouldn't lack conviction,

& get into trouble with
The Tarot instead of
the straight Bull Run,

I fought Olson over
for he wouldn't yield
himself over the number

10, out of my gourd, nuts,
he said I was, not to ground,
but the ground is number 9,

The King of The Mountain,
tested & failing, turgor test,
water, water everywhere, & not

a drop to drink, Aquarian Age,
The Vertical American Thing,
The Spectre of Prophecy before

Sweet Science Reign, Prometheus
Unbound by Shelley before he too
drowned, Romanticism put to bed

in Ishmael's box, Tema. W. Africa,
address all correspondence, like,
you'll be all right, Love.

The Food Problem

for Joanne

That's happened before, & it will
probably happen again, so I
won't worry, Pleistocene Ice
Palace, a better mouse trap
of the years as catches between

Platonic Months of rain, Pluvial
Neanderthal & now, the analytics
of dispersal, as the material went on
to get more holes in it, causing
the shower in other regions to

cough & hack & spit sputum as
big as a Steamer down the drain,
but it was a glorious interglacial
time filled with all sorts of, *every*
convenience imaginable dribbled

from Hainuwele's cunt, till poets,
fearing her parting, reduced it
to a slight discharge, styling
themselves Medicine Men of
this vaginal Milk of Paradise,

wasn't that a great loss, Poetry
Neo Lithique up-tight Ahabic habit
to put-down, except for Keats, such
original voluptuous production, coming
out of the sludge of creation, like

Sargasso Sea, weeds, we are, why
Shakespeare got so angry & then
retired, from such bitching, Marlowe
slain at the stems, The Frond of
The Cocopalm cut up & buried so

men might die & be born again,
it is rather a question of some
occurrence in our cosmos which
mythology expresses equally in
the moon, the woman, & the grain,

the increase of what, as the Elephants
of Atlantis must have cut right through
the labyrinth, Cretan Thallosocracy
sailing around in circles without Wings
of the Dove, Britomartis likewise

after The Flood, The Medi-terranean
World of Sin imposed upon us, here
where the Buffalo roam, & we build
nothing but the Temple of Poseidon
in our hearts, American objects

put back in, Melvillean Things
swallowed up in the Deep Throat of
Oothoon's laughter at the shy spermate-
zoa thinking that makes mammals think
they haven't got enough imagination

to code the code, even Arthurian
with all its half-assed biases knew
better than this fitted &.fitting trip,
symbiotic doesn't cover. The Unknown
is green, Lawrence said, make it up

to you, somehow, we must unhitch
Luvah's Horses from Reason's Chariot
in the Sweet South, domed over by
Pleasure of seeing speech emanate
without thought, but the words

come, themselves, out of same
place, stolen. The Sun was once
inside of, Her, She, the daughter of
Inspiration, comes, directly from
cause, Cleito was her name then,

colonial not clitoral littoral
agitation at the edges, but now
widowy Ameta is making his peace
with Tuwale who will come to Five
Her across these sticks of bamboo.

Buffalo
6.22.74

THE DOG PROBLEM, AUPARISHTAKA

for Diane

She howling in the night will be
the only solution to canine, including
fox, for sure, otherwise, problems
of leaving do arise to darken
the white sheets, new to

the bed of old in which he lay
dying before the same kind
of things he knew were hers
to make good, placed sideways
across the door in the movie

she broke down to get in only
to find him searching the floor
for his scar, or the missing piece
had disappeared into thin air
he thought as she dragged him

from house to house looking
for a telephone, her hold ever
so tight to keep him from bleeding
to death, her motive being
fear of being alone, when

he had only gone out on
the front porch roof through
the window to put up a flag
and set off some fire works
though it was not the 4th of July,

the day he had got married was
long after those curtains caught fire,
she had claustrophobia from being
locked in the closet, or the grandmother
in law had once had an even more

harrowing experience between the mattress
& the springs, so now I don't even
use springs, put the Beautyrest right
on the floor to sleep on the right
side of it facing the woman who

howled on the left, not good to
sleep on the heart, they say,
inverting all laws of matrimony
in bondage to Dog Age time,

I simply won't put up with anymore,
any more than two at a time, is Space
itself, to move, then three came in
to smile the smile, & I knew
the answer again, I could see

in the dark like a cat &
was removed from such numbers,
for she had found a phone &
the neighbors were helpful
& a man with one arm

sewed me up, the right arm
making my initials there, now
I have made my own on the left,
with fire, actually it was heat,
making a sort of crab nebula,

not the tattoo I had thought of
getting, a negation can never
become a contrary & must be
put off continually, told to
go find another, one of the 4

why Poe wanted to eat the teeth,
to show this to everyone, as
Ed said, I mean all of it,
or Harvey reading to the class
of the Whiteness of the Whale,

Albion asleep until his wife
hears the voice of The Bear
in her ear & wants to be
eaten up like the moon was
by someone, other than Fenris.

7.20.74

The Mail Problem

post-poned, for the Wright Sisters

Where is it, you might say, but I drunk
of The Beloved would not, for there is no
other burden, no other you, nor need there be
ever, only the wider recognition as more and
more of you, the many, streaming through,

Orders of Angels to replace Romantic nostalgia
with the actual physical facts pertaining to
separation, contemporary situation to me is
Happy Little Sunbeam, believe it or not, after
all that has transpired between us in

the intervening time, all comes true, dreams
of changing one's self into one's direct contrary,
having a counter, so to speak, to see on display
what one was anyway, Tenderly, it never stops,
what's going on, let go, correlative doctrine to

negative capability, I Get Along Without
You Very Well, no irony, but separating
away the Satanic Surfaces which come
between us, Futurity, the search for it when
it's all over, The Place, a whole 19th C

of it, to occupy the mind, Duality, perplexity
at the slavery of, The Vision, in doubts of
what went on, in Real Life, enough to satisfy
all but the thirst for Ideal Solutions to
problems of this order, the changing of

residence, Bodily Housing, what is the Spirit
that in habits the occasion of fixed Identity,
an extension of Content, made out in Many
Marriages creating The Hierarchy to will
Society into Long-House Form, Novalis' project,

no mimesis or palming off on, the rest of us,
the secret by hanging up, Fulfillingness'
First Finale covers that, without cover, at all,
the five days silence, of the working week,
followed by two days of phantasy & the rest,

deserve what you get, want it, what you gave
must have been, what you wanted, & get
else why would you, take it, to heart when
left or threatened as something, old, or past,
excluded from the running as, Antique,

Full filled all with gems & gold which he by
industry had got, that none his hand dares
stretch touch her Baby form or wrap her
in his swaddling-band, Soft Parental Affection
behind the so-called, Wisdom of the Ages,

Karmic overload, the increasing entropy of
the situation, the Metaphor of the Fan,
so Specialism can never come in & be the
coherent philosophy of the 20th century,
time, time, history, person, society,

politics, space, revolutionary action,
of Earth experience, sex, too, nothing
neglected, as Form, making, it
yield to love, yourself, plying the
pressure, the delivery rate, radical

in what's in, the envelope, The Sheath
lick shut & stamped but not forwarded
for reasons unknown to the addressee,
not arriving here, the box is empty
and the phone rings & no one there,

no matter, She is beautiful in red and
it's time to go out again, each time
a chance for further, speculation
as to what we are, seeking by,
paying such attention to ourselves,

when obviously All's Quiet On The Western
Front & we don't need any more of that
din words were called it being faithful to
the Sumerian accounts of same, The Flood
of correspondence following The Impeachment.

8.3.74

THE BACK PROBLEM

Wampum, for Bonnie Raitt

I have come a long way, Poetry,
& have not thrown my seed into you
for nothing, the heat of your loins
permeating this non-scatological verse
I am making up for your absence

please don't think I think you ever
have abandoned me when The Tables
have been turned, I can hear the roar
of your little motor anywhere, recognizing
your sound, not just the footsteps

coming up the stairs, the moon shining
across the water, golden, a candle blazing
what net, would you do in the same
circumstance what your Grandmother
did, you'd wait too, for the Lizards

to come back out, to support your discipline,
the imaginal as correlative to, the feeling
of desertion, then the old juices flowing
into the conduit of wisdom, Trobriander
ancestress like Edda means that also,

so you have a corroboration from parents
if you have already begun to loosen up
from the bottom of the well where She
first emerged to give the motives & directions
of performance, when they all held to

the bed of Oc as opposite to such information
streaming from ground, out of the repository
of anecdote, held to be valuable in its own
right for the maintenance of societal formality
conducive to stabilities of person & family,

not the Bell System arrangement of time
so the click is lost to the receiver
my Grandfather managed to avoid by
doing it & having it, a white Telephone,
no less, in his dining room, given him

by the Company, starting as a trouble shooter
he had worked his way up to the top
spot & could do everything they asked
of him, except ride with the owner
in his car going over 100 miles an hour,

The God Kings & The Titans, innocent so a lamb
he came to his death, asking me of Frude
& Marx & The Others, as to what they were into,
he had sent me to college & I should know
something, to check out his investment,

waiting until the day of his death to ask
me, who didn't know shit from Shinola
about what he was reading from the paper,
being first a music major & then journalism,
a contradiction, you'd think, in terms, but

I went ahead to talk anyway & he listened,
then taking me aside, from my parents,
said, could you take me home, but I,
fearing my Mother his Daughter, didn't,
& so he decided to split anyway, That Night,

using his foulest language from the Spanish-
American War, freaking my Father, missing
the John, later flailing away at the plastic
of an oxygen tent they had him in, already
interrupted from his spontaneous fetus

on the couch, what a bummer, he had
known he was better off not eating right
quote alone & doing his thing, not likely
he figured to live forever, but certainly
didn't contemplate where to hide the money,

in the fruit room, in cigar boxes, shit,
nothing was found, all go home, diminished
by bent, bent in fact, out of shape, owing
to the same fucking inheritance, no tax
can stop, ought to be a law against, Death.

7.2.74

BEWILDERMENT

for John Wieners & Jackie Bouvier

How to keep things on the track
given all the variables
mumbling & talking to oneself
the maturity of your poems
really the only thing we have
to hold to. Comprehension
    jolts the world again into
    being. I hope so. People so
don't know it has been made,
like a poem. Nothing changeable
you are not plugged in. You can
survive without it. Bowels
move without Exlax America
relax let go of Columbus
    John has already died
    his hairs red & yellow
to catch a fellow. My memory
refuses to recollect further evidence,
which you only mistake for idiosyncrasy.
My anger gets the best of me
& I cannot write. Only honor
please what I cannot ignore,
Her coming in the door.

2.3.75

IMMORTALITY TO BE ACHIEVED BY GODS NOT OF THE UNDERWORLD

for Ed Sanders

the air of heaven here
with us, nebulous as dust
from Coalsack Bluff, Ragnarok sense
of End of World, Her fragrance
replacing the sun
     even our own dear own
mounds become a cloud of dust
Novalis novelty necessary, and Right
Reason to field it, in heat of the furnace
the structure of imagery intact
      fresh from the ice
   as One Man, standing by a burning bush
   during the Occultation proclaimed a New Law,
   Mumbo Jumbo Time, as much as the situation
   would bear
      emergence from the past as magnetic
      mesh—ninety degree
      phase shift—
      the degradation of the herm, personal
      topos. into *psychopompos*

      so the whole thing
   has had to shift from heroes, kings,
   & quests, Indo-Euro-pean Amarna Age incest
   replacing the ancient Osirian West,
   the eater of the eater, Death

Strong or Elohistic
hence in no need of intensification
or old Crane Dance labrys method
of the Niners, as Quetzalcoatl himself
images his own "Flowering War"

figures anyway
from Sphinx to Centaur, of God &. the World—
which is behind you, when you put it there—
thus the history of philosophy, the mapping
of the void
           Orpheus including
Mimir with his singing head
the bowling ball that hits
the nine pins, funerary games
severed heads of the Great Cave

March 1975

Man Is Interesting

to Lewis MacAdams

Have what you crave
but remember to test
your limits, so

you redeem the past,
The Dead from despair
of Futurity unleashed,

The Dogs upon us all,
even to gobble-gang point
of Pound's picnic, you

must have The Vent,
which means to be rich
as hell, as all

knots are a wall
ready to be shot open, Lew,
where has your method gone?

check it out, next
time those 3 won't offer
anymore until you provide

that particular thing that's
going on, & make a mess of
it, except the Emanative

Joy, which is larger now
than life, if you have to
beat up the poor with

Baudelaire, go ahead but
the Memory of what was
before or after only

gets you more Self-
Confidence in something
you're out of, a womb,

Man, coming down into it,
The Necessary Angel even,
if it's poetry, & you

haven't left anything out,
specifically, or made
a mistake about the other

side of the argument which
will never resolve itself
into any other or subside

by doing it, to make it
come true, the good will
you always had anyway

there is a way out, pray
God, there is another
axis, if you follow me,

until the female show
herself you want to
screw, so spiritually

the best thing post-
Blake is Olson because
of his insistence being

so directed as to appertain
directly to what most of us
are born of, a dispensation

easily arouses apathy if not
out & out antipathy, as Duncan
has had to stress, coming from

New England, true, born you is,
of your Mother as you are via
the part playing in it, of

Your father, the return Up
the tree is as decisive as
it is silly for you to stay

up waiting for her to call
when you know she won't,
throughout All Eternity

I bless you, you bless me,
5-anki das, and again ten
times he took her, the fucking

of the mountain, with his mind
with the rock he slept, 10-
anki das, closer to Corbin

than ever before, I wish
you had given back Hawkes &
Frankfort sooner, the way

the West was won, nothing
like Today's Journalism
makes out, a pair of Texas.

6.17.74

ODE TO CUPID   DOUBLE SONNET

The Veil, you must have The Veil, & it is
black, without which The Tree of Mystery
goes up in smoke, don't be stupid, as
Khusraw spied Shirin at her bath & was
forever blinded, a little bit of green
lace is all you need, Do Not Strike At
The Face, Persian Miniature Imperative
circa 1520 as sure as you sent me reeling,
not the same as Medicine Wheel spinning,
to be spun in the Sweet South, Reason's
Domain, veritas, the Fourth Musketeer
blundering his way to Victory, Indomitable,
Sirhan Sirhan the Middle Voice of Doom
stuttering stag pursued by Hounds of Heaven,
where the fish swim backwards, up stream
or across as Robt Duncan sd he wld when
he no longer stood in Her Way, impediments,
but O Siduri, The Shadowy Eighth is a door
in itself, made of wood of Forests of Night
Dante saw from which to escape, Brand brand
new nuova, bless you, Lawrence movie maker
for Women in Love, & men, too, Harvey loved,
this is my answer, no Crystal Cabinet maker,
at this point in the story you do change
horses in the middle of the stream, &. get
the message across, I take my hat off, To
the Ice Man frozen in his own juices, justice
reigns, & not by going back to the pre-Qedipal.

7.5.74

STATISTICS OF THIS, CUBITS, DUST

I'D SURE LIKE TO BE AROUND, I'll tell you that, I've had enough splitting to last a life time. Death is not the limit it used to be when I was young and had no notion of living less than forever as a formal category of hope. And I certainly do still hope, hope we'll be together in this new way, squandering identity to prove manhood can compete with truncation's apathy, a variegated hue, not color of the Rainbow View. The material we have in common will be transported from here to there, so don't worry, just bring it all with you to the exclusion of knowing so it can't be used by anyone again, as before, to set us back. Virtuous, yet easily used by the Others; thus Gypsies got put down for driving such hard bargains off the backs of their wagons when they came to town. It is always the same with you, not knowing before when the seed would grow to flower, power in us to determine vision of geologic origins, whereby you get the message, so what is twined can be as fabulous as it was the first time, the bridge over which the Enchanted Pony passes, which will serve you well when all the drums are still and there seems no way, save conjuring, for the world to right itself, from wrong.

He first asked each, "Did you come out of time of trouble the humble way?" And if any had used their power wrongly he refused them admittance to the settlement. He was slow to decide, for he had sent his wife away in accordance with prophecy until the Great Biomorphism has ended. This meeting will show physics of affection, the way things feel, humanly. Back behind, on the other side, the mathematics of history, the previous job, if speech is quick to render, otherwise whistling in the dark. A mood of parental guidance, climbing the stairs to witness the primal scene again rather than descending to profession of ancestral conviction the real matter outside projected apace. Jumping to the conclusion of Dream before awaking to meaning: it must not be allowed to accumulate again, eat your words, and mine, as his. This is our Sweet Sciences and one arrives at Turtle Island sooner, or later when he does not, desire it.

Statistics of this, cubits, dust, theoretically immaculate, non-nuclear conception of starwater Great Lakes spore, so to make a dwelling place of differences, so one of each, from here to Tule. The gig, temporary, to yield prior Hiberion matters discoverable through contact with ridges. No longer a Great Wheel revolving, industrial analysis of pre-lunar calibration of the fundamental contours of area, dry land at the next level without fencing, physiognomic circumference of each ex-pression, shifts the diluvial axis. I don't know how also to say it today, forsaking all Others, she who wears the flute lapel who will enter through this talking leaf, hear her arrival.

THE ESCHATON: RESURRECTION OF THE BODY
(TO CLEAR N.O. BROWN)

Now consciousness as that other no data distraction.
No healing medicine man Shaw-man son above trauma down.
    No bull roaring to the rescue; to open a wound no
longer there birth is not asleep & a forgetting.
    No recollection but all the while going forth
returning (viz the last plate of *Jerusalem*) no where
Tro-phonian labour only the movement matters stirs itself
the initiating form. The conventional location: Earth.
No machination, machine-metal need now no murder Cain able
to brook all Adam's horizontalism a case of mistaken identity:
a maze, a labyrinth come through, like a sock pulled through
we thought we could put it on we could the metallurgists dream:
3 astro-nauts burned up: projects Mercury, Apollo, Gemini.
    Like Pandora's box good & evil (Equivocal worlds)
    or like: Hell is, a very curious formal designation.
Who goes there? H & other tricksters. Back & forth.
    No necessary angel. We opened our veins solely to know.
On this side of ANW, was it, their pity, such an error.
Yes, always. Thus March. & every other Felix Culpa. He
came to take away the Remembrance, of sin. That is all.
The fermenting Corn at Eleusis, sclerosis of the Promethean
liver. Sublimity, mystery, alchemy.
    No heroes dying to be reborn. Born dead. To that,
gravity. He reconciled to it. You're here, the eternal life.
Pants down, Earthlings. Emaculate conception. No
Oedipus, no Sphinx, no Freud, no original sin or sickle.

Those bright guys (Quetzalcoatl, et al.) are out of business,
& I'll bet they're glad, to get off the hook. They've been
carrying us long enough. Living out that cosmic error:
        hands, wands, swords—whatever instrumentation,
        as atomic power is, the last act of smiths.
We are the instruments now, oh Lucy Melos. No machines of a y
kind. All turned serpent inside out, shedding backwards—
9 times. The labyrinthine thread, Ariadne (see Graves) to
find your way. No Tao, Tys, Zeus . . . . .

WHERE THE SICKLE WAS LEFT THERE BE GRASS BURNING
This will be the third possible
(3)   coherence: Animal–Angel–Radical
            $mc^2 = hf$ /   Aquarius-Uranus-ecstasy-as effective
(Everybody shall have all of the money; what is consumed)
Feed–back (supra McLuhan):   the whole public domain: you become
what you behold.   El-ectrification accomplished: fire-water for
all. You are redeemed & initial as having been you. America
is now visionary. Pay attention to all organized things, e.g.
John Wieners.

Or, like, can you remember, before the fusion—when the
welding took place, when you were forged, phylogenetically,
run out. ACID burns through, down to, reduces, as corrosive method.
Such remembrance cuts through does not renew ancestral voices
prophesying war; before war, was peace, was animal angel peace,
organic novelty, God, walking with man in paradise apple orchard
ocean island continent—in the sense that they did observe a cosmic
position and attitude which no longer is a condition of deviation
for present man: hence, present form must extend from present content.

Or, further, that, *crucially*, the whole thing now becomes
the furnace of affliction, we can press people, to the point
that, the original gift of heat from those titanic figures
(or like Nephilim?) is no longer the spoils of War (to build
heaven in hell's respite: i.e., sublimation— the thing driving
the whole thing is now busted).

Therefore, no messenger, guardian, go-between shaman, magician, priest, doctor, analyst, after the fact (of Kronos's knife, of castration complex, etc.).   You are the between, the middle voice of it all, the present presence, during the peace.   During is a verb. *You are already twice-born as having been born into this Aryan angel age.* Society is no longer a 2nd womb which to be reborn by some rebirth strategy.   It itself is transformative.   *To enter into* that *is* an initiative immediately— a processing by best Whitehead definition. A true psychic processional: if you can acquire proper attention, I mean, dig, be aware of such phi-unit order. No intermediary links: it is all in the middle, the hermetic middle voice of the animate creation. No Reilley no Cocktail Party, no El-iot, no totem master, no mush. SEA-Change, the primes of which are the going on. The door has been removed, hinges & all. There never was an opening that way. Either the whole thing is the passage or no. It ain't made until everybody makes it. That the Last Judgment.   Together. (Blake: They conversed in visionary forms dramatic . . . . .). All atl atl watl water flow el-ectric flow. Water the best conductor, like Hermes orichalcum wand, the body is itself 90 some per cent H20, the Electron flow of events in this electromagnetic epoch. No temenos. It is all the incorporation. No threats, no treats. Tropology is truth. Tree-duro: to be made permanent. "Who dwell by the edge of the sea"

Just to discover your own animal/angel
you, tutelary spirit you literal like cave animaux
or the Bible says to be you the real you
is to be angel, you Aquarius Angel / Uranos &

Gaia
together in a happy population under the
sun: no secret sex death darkness, taboo.
That is not man's nature, though it ishu–man nature: Tiger, Tiger.
(Then God said, my spirit shall not
shield (abide in) man for ever, since he is but flesh:

let the time allowed him to be number 12,000 years.)

Lion   &   Lamb
Christ, first risen of the dead.

Now the two come together:

No Father but . . . . Heaven

8   *Christ*, the middle voice

T = cross

No Mother but . . .   Earth

John Clarke, Penny Rodefer, Stephen Rodefer, Pauline Butling,
Charles Olson, and John Wieners at Onetto's in Buffalo, c.1963

SEVEN SONNETS IN THEIR SEQUENCE
WRITTEN SEPTEMBER 29, 1976

Law-Giving

We must see clearly the ruiner
of ancient Greece, Zeus-Jupiter,
how he became pulled away from
his original perfective action, one's own
lord & Lot of Doom, the dawning
upon oneself of oneself, or Urizen
as Truth-Dream before Luvah stole
the Horses of the Sun, what befell
Our Don of Phoenician Minoa when
Indo-European Mycenean emissaries of
conjugal love, having no sense of west
knocked out their Sixth Eye of God, the rest
is history until Jesus came to remove
this imposture of Patriarchal Pillars & Groves.

The Only Way

for Dorn

Cain forgives Able, Claggart forgives Billy Budd,
the K he slew in his dark self-righteous pride
must become his own dear twin brother,
even that hard-hearted tyrant Zeus himself,
if he is ever to get his speech flowing again,
can you stand to see this monster & not want
to kill it, yuk, or do you so love it you're afraid
it will be killed, by someone else, who could
kill Ulikummi except Enki, & what does it mean
to be translated into a Blue Star, why is it such
a secret in the West still, Orphic wouldn't you say,
or like Lohengrin, to keep from her his original,
exactly who do you think that other guy was in
Shakespeare's Sonnets, wasn't he a huge twin to Will.

At Long Last

Why was it Gilgamesh went on quest for
immortality, was it not because of the death
of Enkidu at the hands of Inanna, but that always
happens when patriarchal propaganda has made
you afraid of her, who can withstand her power
but this can't go on, Siduri will find you at some
bar & open the gate for you, the Shadowy Eighth or
both the K & yourself transcended & ready for *Origin*
a magazine of the creative, where you are going to fall
asleep, & dream such an alcheringa it will seem
as plain as day. so much so that you will even break
the oldest taboo in the world, you will give the woman
at the well your words, John Golden Mouth restored
to human society which is a city yet a woman, Jerusalem.

Bad Bed, Hesiod

On first looking out through Athena's eyes,
or the lamb emerging out through the gates
of her poor broken heart, the kourotrophos
the Society of Eternal Events, Herakles in drag,
or sperm-brain *Basileus Albina*, Lost Phoenician
Original in the West where phallic pomp & pride
ruined discourse, so we can only stammer
in the face of bitchy accusations, or get angry
& hit, at least Melville got it as far as the K
& not his wife, the next step in this working out
of projection would be to put him to work, to direct
his anger as Blake did his Spectre, against the real
enemy, those who would depress mental & prolong
if they could corporeal war forever, pure animosity.

FUCK YOU

If Archie Bunker promises Edith he won't
throw his back anymore, & if Gore Vidal
rescues Mary Hartman from the mental hospital
these are beginnings, by analogy, of Brotherhood
that is of being projective in the Human Universe
sense, not saving women, protecting women, or
any previous program, but imply entering
that world, of Power, of Britomartis & Sophia
the living & the dead, to be able to speak
as a Don to Portia, the vocal event that
consumes all space-time, that dumps the two
Platonic Months, & restores the I-am-Rig-you-are-
Veda discourse of Heaven & Earth, Heavenly Ava
Earthy Oly the inversion of sun & moon story.

Patriarchy there, Matriarchy here

The dipolar, & the great biomorphic loss,
which is the Secret of the West, well-kept,
Eden, all perverted, reflected in the Veg
glass, mimetic fallacy of all looking
at the picture, what Gawain knew, you don't
get to speak to the King without going through
the Queen, which Lance seems to have literalized
like all of us adulterous pricks, & ruined society
called Camelot one of the better Muslim shots
in the West, for the Sexes, yes, indeedy, but why
should the K be allowed to trick us this way
& for so long, never mind, more to the point, isn't it
true that Trickster figure is just a vulgarization of
the Angelophany itself, of Hainuwele's terrestrial animal

THE LEOPARDS OF CATAL HUYUK

Underestimated, wild, feral, beasts
wheeling variously according to size of
birth, no society except for milk
bearing tree, they are one, we are many,
if we try to be so, we get the ultimate
anguish, one law for lion & ox, if they try
to be many, astrologists all, society
collapses, didn't mean to drone on about
this but She is coming, the Amazon Achilles
killed & it will happen again in Aquarius
if now everybody doesn't change, get
Paul Bunyan to build Golgonooza with
an ox & pickaxe, not out of Hainuwele's
limbs, like that Marduk, trying to replace Enki.

AT THE EDGE OF SILENCE

THE ARABS KNOW THE FOUR AXES: earth/sky city/language. The center of Islamic reverence is the *Q'abah* (cube), temple built about a meteorite. The falling star. In their desert, the Angel Gabriel was real, for earth and sky had something to do with each other. Not as we think, that *city* and sky, our Babylonian skyscrapers have to do. What they had to do with each other, earth and sky took place in silence. Out of that silence, God's silence, they would say, came finally language. Gabriel speaks "in the name of God" (bismillahi ullahh.) For the universe is silent and language is human dance.

The Q'uran is center of Arab language as the Q'abah is to their orb. Mohammad was an orphan. His family, tribe. He was illiterate. His language begins with him. His language, the people. They shared it. Nomad. The city is full of remembrances, the womb of "wisdom" babble. The language of the Arabs is born of a father silence, and a rustling mother, humans and animals doing what they must to survive. This language is lightning. Not light. Moving on. Weightless. And after lightning then, only later, thunder. A long drawn out sigh. It is there even to my ignorant ear in the sharp consonants and the long breathing vowels.

The heavens are not stars. "They" is sky. Clear. Translucent. Like sea. The Arabs were, I think, privileged to see the union of sky and earth because they lived at the edge of silence. They were privileged to see language born out of dying cities, Byzantium to the north, Alexandria to the south, Babylon to the east, Greece to the southwest. India off at the edge of the world. The Fertile Crescent, already a smoldering dust bowl. They were the survivors of Sodom & Gomorrah, they did not look back, they wished oasis.

Desert has always seemed to me geometrical. Really, the measure of earth. Because in the desert the microcosm and the macrocosm meet.

Spring comes to the desert so you can see it, petal by petal, hue by hue, leafbud showing itself to human eyes. After World War I, the Banu Howeitat moved north looking for graze for their camels. They were able literally to measure the pace of spring as the 50,000 of them moved north in a line said to be 50 miles wide, 5 miles a day. Till they came to the border of Syria, that imaginary creation. Were forbidden to cross the border. Watched the line of spring move on, their camels starve. Milk dry up. Much talk with the "great powers" and finally they were allowed to move north, too late. Such confrontations with the city-dwellers' sense of earth were frequent. City as straitjacket. Those "geometrical" boundaries, like our sections, lots and suburbs which are the most evident opposition to any true measure of the earth.

The lesson for-language was also, or has become for me at least, that language has no history other than that which we allow it to have. Or can, perhaps, be made anew each day, a new home, minimal.

When they speak of Arab science they mean astronomy geography. Very similar. Naming the nameless stars and delineating the boundless earth. We must indeed guide ourselves with maps but not confuse them with the earth the sky. The Arab following a map, an itinerary will always know there is more. We do not often remember that. It will become what you discover it to be.

The Q'uran is a book of praises and curses. Praises and curses are the wands of power and magic language. It is the Arab's counter to the power of megalith the power men have over those hives built on earth where the earth is now only a ghost. Praises that the earth flourish and curses that the cities die. They cannot be separated, "God" (silence) through Gabriel (intellect) to Mohammed (language) swears by the land, the dawn, the sun, the night, the blood-clot, daybreak, the earthquake, the sand dunes and builds the new city the Islamic community out of nature, those parameters, bounds beyond us, which really do surround us.

Is it inhuman?! Vexy likely. Is it human? Very likely arbitrary. Meaning a kind of innocence which is no more than ignorant. What, one learns from the Arab innocence is to simply "protect" oneself as little as possible. Billowing clothes, billowing homes. Isomorphism. Calligraphy like planetary orbits, or high grasslands. Movements like fissures in sandstone, like hawks a swooping circle, give in to the pressures you can, *islam*, clear your head of fantasy and human arrogance. It is not "our" earth & sky. It is our language and city we build as best we can.

FIRE DELIGHTING IN ITS FORM:
NOTES ON MYTH

D ISTINGUISH MYTHOLOGY: stories of God's & heroes from God
as organ of novelty: creative advance (Cosmology).

Coming of corrupters: fallen angels/titans—this disrupted
process; brought gifts beyond the capacities of earth–flesh–garden:
FIRE. But if these 'heroes' ain't it; neither is Yahweh (Ya–hoo)—man,
which was Swift's point: it has been ex-*cre*-mental. Shit. The story is
very confused: *crea*tion (actually what followed the trauma/serpent
catastrophe) Elohim on water (which follows the stars throwing down
their spears & watering heaven with tears—Blake's Tyger says it all): in
equivocal worlds things are equivocal: only hope remained, after the box
had opened: question remains as to good & evil—these Promethean
(trickster) gifts of the serpent (Quetzalcoatl) Hermes-tree of knowledge,
etc., seemed good to some bad to others—mankind has been sacrificing
the world to himself ever since: it is now time for the ultimate sacrifice?
The Secret of the West. See Shelley's P.U. Love not War, the curse

Hence, the crucial immersal now: can't take side in this old war busi-
ness; of gods & heroes, shit:

> For those the Race of Israel oft forsook
> Their living strength, & unfrequented left
> His righteous Altar, bowing lowly down
> To Bestial Gods.
>   PL

> (also Blake on beginning of religion in MHH)

Too long, the good guys & the bad guys, Urizen & Orc: in endless
cycles of Ulro: the uroboric serpent: on the Tree of Mystery: always the

same: eternal death: the phylogenetic strain: crime-cream-creation-corruption: attempting to become more than man, we become less. Luvah/love.

The Reprobate addresses the Redeemed not the Elect: so long as there is guilt man will continue to repress all energy, i.e., kill himself, if he is the last bit left: hence the necessary separation: to distinguish the form of his own energy from that old serpent residue.

In other words, we are back in phase with the rest of the universe: so that now the very things that were productive of the most evil (error), & were therefore forbidden by the Elect, for their own protection, are now possible—the need for those taboos, etc., is removed, because now man can in fact accomplish them in the flesh, in the body-mind organism he is, the incarnation is complete & is now moving toward daily consummation—if we remain bound to the old laws (whether negative (Mosaic) or positive (Hermetic) we shall lose completely, because this is the age of the promised return, of last judgment, of fire—so that in fact it is no longer the case of Prometheus; he shall be unbound: no longer monstrous forms, titanic forms, unnatural, hybrid, half-man, half-animal, etc. Now finally crucially human morphology: fire delighting in its form. Word/flesh. (history-logos-time congruent to living strength/flesh). We had 9 jumps, nine serpent-cat lives ahead; & had to suffer it through; the 'deluge' of matter, from their point of view, those aliens, who came into this darkness, & had to suffer it out (tla-atl): before once more action was equivalent to known form, & one could do what one knew, like knowing how to fly but not being able to.

The will must not be bent except in the day of divine power!

Time is the mercy of eternity: only a temporary measure. The eternals pull up their tent, break off relation, cut down the tree-of-life, eternal life, retired to mountains-sky, etc., (man expelled from the garden) now time is finished. That's what the apocalypse & last judgment mean, that the covering cherub, the guard at the Western gate, is removed, burnt up, displaying the infinite that was hid. That Christ made it possible for the whole planet (Pisces) & now in Aquarius it does pour equal, electromagnetically.

The divided/dual-nature, the gap, has finally been closed, come together, andro-gyne Makroanthropus. Christ by the term of himself made it possible for all. But now no *imitatio* anybody, you are the initiation as having been born after & into, this as affective epoch. The Form of the Real was revealed by his action, was the radical of his action here: history re-created: number: now the creative advance again goes on in us because we can receive it, if we choose to, no longer hung, behind ourselves by being ahead, & so always letting the process go in preference for some higher activity: now we can tune in direct, having caught up to ourselves: it is in that sense that the fall was an aspiration; & the redemption of going-down;

Which is why it becomes so much a matter of stamina of being able to stay with it, with the things, of the presence to be made permanent by articulation. Size. Literal; radical; numeral. Don't be afraid. No longer birth, a sleep & a forgetting. The marriage of heaven & earth: the eternal return: Albion & Jerusalem, a city yet a woman: anima mundi, the fourth which comes out of the three: Zoa-Cherubim powers hum on.

A Sheaf of Poems 2

BEGINNING WITH THE GAS STATION AT THE END OF PAPA'S DRIVE

Henry Morrison Flagler
   married Stephen Harkness's niece
         of Bellevue
     her uncle
       gave John D. Rockefeller
          some bread to begin
THE STANDARD OIL COMPANY OF OHIO
      complete & worldwide
        by 1869
   based on the rebate, Flagler the "dynamo"
      of the new outfit
The South Improvement Company
         John D. (Baptist) was shocked
        at the violent reaction
        competition equaled waste
The Parliament of Petroleum
    1879
The Tidewater Pipe Line Company
    1881
"They are mighty smart men, I guess if you ever had to
deal with them you would find *that* out." —

       Commodore Vanderbilt's son
      William, as to his reasons for
     granting rebates to Standard
now on Pearl St., NYC

The first American trust
>   (July 23 1892 Alexander Berkman
>   plugs Frick; Jay Gould dies)

Backtrack: 1851   *Moby Dick*
>   "centralization"
>   v.s.
>   Herbert Spencer
>   "life is a jungle"
>   "survival of the fittest"
Between the end of The Civil War
& the end of the Century
>   Americans bought
two hundred million copies
>   of Horatio Alger Jr.

>   competition was disorder

March 21 1892   Sherman Act
>   complied with (in Ohio)
THE STANDARD OIL COMPANY OF NEW JERSEY
>   becomes holding company
>   John D. "retires" to Tarrytown
>   1896
>   John D. Jr. enters NYC office
>   1897
>   the utter absence of chance
>   Henry Flagler becomes
>   "godfather of Florida"

>   1911
>   U.S. Supreme Court dissolves
>   STANDARD OF N.J.

Result: 38 separate STANDARD Oils!
>   April 21 1914

The Ludlow Massacre
John D. Jr. shocked
hires 'Poison Ivy' Ledbetter Lee
to clean image
(shiney-dime idea)
The Foundation
John D. Sr. dies
1937 (age 98)
leaving
ONE BILLION DOLLARS
(he had cried only twice
at-the passing of his wife,
& when the homestead was torn down

1969
EXXON
puts it all back together
to continue original plan
complete & worldwide
ORDER

Note" All of this might possibly have been averted
had John D.'s father
not had to leave Tioga Country in the first place.
Evidently there was a warrant out
for his arrest on charges of "fooling
around"

Jimmy says
"Don't be foolish"
I agree
I still owe them $300
Papa, of course, paid back.

All Fucked Up, But Why?

Transfer of power, what
guard of Tartaros, what
station, what the hammer
& the chain, disdain her

who wept & went home as
much as she could have
promised something more
than she did, get sore

over nothing, placement
of goods, stolen, rent
deposit has not come back,
Nixon still on the rack,

I'm no good at this, wait
a minute, something might
break, net another day
another dollar, hut pay

dues, non-Union, scat gig,
this office of intrigue
shouldn't go to anybody
who doesn't want to study

the situation, steady work
for the ridiculous clerk,
listing things not to do
but look at, out of the blue

comes the answer, ejaculate
the Universe, at any rate
self-action of his *vertu*,
the root of all evil, Hughes

to appear, calm & collected,
the new regime unelected,
to do dirtier tricks of state,
O how hard it is to wait

for the call to come, Kennedy
waiting for the word, Sunset Bay
is OK now but what about after
December, will a boat leave for

Africa? it's all so up in the air
wonder, will we even be there
for the Fair has Atlantis already
arisen, whither is my lucid melody?

Inauguration Day 1974

Why I Wouldof Probably Won't Now
Support George McGovern for President

"I know a wind in purpose strong
it spins *against* the way it drives"
—Herman Melville, *The Conflict* of *Convictions 1860-1*

because obviously now what The Eagle experienced is
contrary to what apparently The Gov believes does he?
at any rate acted upon in response to whatever it was
the one and only (sole) preparation a contemporary man
of political bent has open to him to qualify himself
for higher public office as every Man-On-The-Street knows
but for all the talk about is still as much ignored
in favor of that abstraction Public Opinion as before
and so the forces of evil read entropy wins again and
the system goes on continues to run down what a shame
in this case! here it was the chance to reverse the old
Wheels politics as simple mimetic practice as Melville
as early as 1851 spotted that much prior to The Origin
of the Species "post-mortem effects" Lawrence called them
what a shame not to have felt that new wind in purpose
strong Mac Govern wrong and should take the blame for
what is about to happen to America because there isn't
time to judge effects anymore only time to Tell-It-Like-
It-Is it is serious Business we are about to begin and
could have used such help as Convention allows *but* now
it is over before it's begun and again we lose precious
time the very thing we could most use that's how it works
history what a pity not to have foresight Mighty Mac G
given your history you should have flown with The Eagle
this time into the highest office of The Land but no you

chickened out you were afraid someone was shitting you
about the future where The Nation was concerned and how
you were going to have to go too! to the very place where
The Eagle has been! but The Eagle didn't tell you he thot
you knew and/or if you didn't he knew if he did you wouldn't
so he thot okay maybe this way *but* it didn't work Dr. Mac
couldn't quite get his shit together in time he needed more
now he has plenty four more years to sit read *shit* & brood
like his bro Mac Arty how stupid can you get to throwaway
such opportunity so easily for change like the guy in that
Sufi story when it's time to go and he's been waiting for
years misses the boat at the last minute because he can't
quite part with his "cabbage" it's too heavy for words and
stinks when left behind the STORY you can't change it is
history only *and* the best way to check that out is to sort
of try to remember the last time you were able to erase same
except by the way The Eagle has already done See him soar
way up there above the Missouri (Misery) Barnyard see Him
glide alone above not needing even the Beautiful Orange-
Eyed Smelly Monster he knows where he's going not back to
that place where he's been we've all been Outer Space? *no*
he's ahead of the game 6 yrs. ahead as we all are *except*
the forces that seek to govern by capitalizing on the Lag
except it won't work anymore they have exposed themselves
and are no longer invisible we all know them quite well
and further KNOW they have no power or authority of their
own *but only* what they sponge off the rest of us *anyone*
who would fail to answer the call of The Eagle or call it
Depression *irony* the cure SHOCK how shocking must it get
before these Druids SEE The Earth is not their stamping
ground but belongs to at least if not us Humans Lord
Poseidon power of gravity itself the only (sole) way of
experiencing the flight of The Eagle read negative entropy
or capability (Human) as John Keats M.D. called it who knew
what it was to be DE-PRESSED and how to get it over with
that is over *to* the other side *Hyperion* part of the story
he didn't get time to finish it too bad we can't finish it
for him *no* this is a decided set-back not to mention the
obvious gain from exposure because it isn't at all that

interesting or kindly taken to and *no one* deserves it Death
made so easy Political Suicide enough said Save The Eagle
The American Eagle!

Special to No *Count Medicine*
by Field of Mars Correspondent
Paul Revere August 1st 1972

And as of Aug 1
let the message go out
to any who would balk

"Lie not one to another,
seeing that ye have put off
the old man with his deeds."
Col. 3 : 9

THE MARTIAN STATUTES—SONNET

We must remember not everyone
has a red wagon to remember
the famous 'Basque difference' as
The Original Ax fell on Mars' birthday
the anti-matter within creation like
star-water story hydrogen & carbon
make oil The Black Gold to measure
extent of red streak Quetzalcoatl's
beard *uraidu* The Dawn of The Gods
my notes say somewhere buried in
my files The Rottenness in Denmark
Bylebyl's translation says shall yield
to The Red Intelligence Jack Ruby shooting
Oswald then dying of cancer part of the plan.

10.20.74

The Horned Gate of True Dreams

actually Jung
  but this is nothing new
because he held out
  for the "firmness"
   of the figures
    like, *anima*
as such
   even though he may not
   have, except through
   Toni Wolff, known
   any but the negative
   aspects of desire
   as dream falsely
   considered so
   as to cluster
   around the edges
   thus obscuring by
   projection as in
   a mirror what was
   at the center
   of his stand-point

    "firmly held"
   as if I'm quoting someone
    then, like the corn
    is held to be

"Eternal"
in the sense of
"never sown"
meaning the future
is the planted path
not the past
which is why
it's unreapable
why Hesiod
& others say
"unharvested"
except Homer's
prophecy, that the oar
will be mistaken
for the winnowing
thing
whatever it's called
eventually,

anyway, Her imperishable descent
is what is held to
even if only
in glimpses
you see her
directionally accurate
at least
not from before
what you've known
from birth
already, always
in the dog's mouth
the moment
you enter hell
or think to

take or give
something
that doesn't belong
to you, as yourself
enterable etc. but
to the whole future
        "archetype" as such
            of the world
                better

B. Cass Clarke, Robin Blaser, and John Clarke, Buffalo, 1985

OLSON

The Metaphysics of Survival

For anyone living in this century it has been a matter of survival. We live in, as D.H. Lawrence put it, the post-mortem effects of the sinking of the Pequod.

In his third Charles Olson Memorial Lecture last month (March, 1988), "Poetic Reality & Market Realities," Allen Ginsberg brought up the word trust as a term of both. What we had put our trust in, like his lady in Dallas with the white luggage, has not held. As example of poetic reality he invoked Walt Whitman's adhesiveness or comradeship. "Otherwise, Rome."

I was thinking of Ishmael's touching of another's hand while kneading the sperm of a whale, "unawares," that word of Coleridge's, and Olson's bumping of flesh on a bus in the Yucatan, when I heard Allen saying: Nothing lasts forever . . . maybe we're on the way out."

Lawrence had considered that possibility in a poem published in *Pansies* in 1929. The poem ends in three questions: Must we hold on? Or can we now let go? Or is it even possible we must do both?

Allen had earlier quoted Gregory Corso saying, "If you have a choice, choose both," so I was already carrying that word "both" when I remembered the Lawrence poem (pensée).

Olson, in a poem of 1946, unpublished until last year's *Collected Poems*, titled "Canto One Hundred and One," dated "november 22" (now an important date in what Rimbaud designated a "time of assassins"), also found himself using the word "both," and, as you might expect, in all caps. The poem begins with the lines: The earth is for the living OR the earth is the dead man's land. BOTH depending upon the way you look at it.

The poetic thought contained in the word both will become a key to Olson's projective enterprise. As Blake had prospectively formulated it before the Pequod went down, 1851: "Without contraries is no progression." In the Spring of that year (1946), Olson, in "La Preface," had made the connecting link with the lines:

We are born not of the buried but these unburied dead crossed stick, wire-led, Blake Underground
>The Babe
>>the Howling Babe

It is often said that Olson came to poetry late, after the war, after politics, but actually his sense of a poetic reality was forming early. A Notebook entry for February, 1933 (Olson was 22 years old) reads: "He who sets to poetry picks up a white feather blown from the fowl of Heaven." In his Olson lecture Allen was forced by his topic to a more available analogy. To his own question: "Where do you get that trust?" he said: "Maybe like in AA—hit bottom and come back up." (For more on this procedure see Gregory Bateson's important essay on AA.) Olson's own even more available bottom is to be found in a poem of 1942, also included in the *Collected*, called "Ballad for Americans," ending with these lines:

> I could tell you a story
> it ain't in the books
> What do you say about my woman's looks?
> that's important, see
> I'd always won until she licked me,
> yeah,

she gave me the gettysburg

> get it? (swing it)
> I got a history
> you got a history
> the South's got a history
> and we'll all get a history when we get the gettysburg!

If such losses as Viet Nam or now the so-called Crash do not provide entry into history, even the way here indicated may be baffled as well by common cause, made smaller and thus cheaper by familiarity.

The poem "Troilus" from the play of the same name, 1948 (*The Fiery Hunt and Other Plays*), points to the problem:

That love at least must live
is lie we practice to protect
what we inherit, breath,
unwilling to admit
the large wrongs bring
love also down to
death.

A Notebook entry for March 2, 1935—Olson is 24—contains an out-
line and notes for a short story or novel to be called "A Plague on This
Your House," whose concluding section concerns "the final woman,"
and his note to himself is: "find more about her." Then he writes: "Wil-
liam Blake—only man ever solved it . . . Katharine could be the earth
woman & nothing else." Meaning, I take it, he (Blake) didn't need to
get a "man" from her, he was one, but something else, and I don't mean
"Muse" either, but something poets since have gone to them for, and a
few others, but not too many professors—who Olson says on the next
page "are as bodyless and dead as French aristocrats."

Lawrence's poetic reality of BOTH, as he said of Whitman's Open
Road, is "a morality of actual living, not of salvation," that is, not
survival as salvation. Likewise, once Olson discovered he had a history
or that his own history included such antithetical action, it is no longer
of concern, as Lawrence says, that "the sinking of the Pequod was only
a metaphysical tragedy after all. The world goes on just the same." A
trusted local, or what he will later call "haunts and habits" and "cave of
being"—and here he would prefer the word *ethics* to Lawrence's "moral-
ity"—can constitute poetic reality in the *same place* where Eliot had seen
only the "Hollow Men" of Allen's market realities. The standard confu-
sion here, as for example Coppola's use of Eliot in *Apocalypse Now*, is
with images of apparent loss of place and person having to stand in for
present poetic reality, as though nothing were real except what can be
validated against that backdrop of the "unburied dead."

The real dead, the unmetaphoric dead, "The Dead," the ones of value,
take place with the living, in the place of BOTH—to stay with that
neutral, methodological word a bit longer before allowing it to yield to
SPACE, the word perhaps most associated with Olson. You who come
after us you who can live when we are not make much of love.

This is the opening of "Only the Red Fox, Only the Crow," a poem of 1948 you may remember from *The Archaeologist of Morning*. The lines I wanted to quote are:

> And when, on summer field
> two horses run for joy
> like figures on a beach
> your mind will find us,
> as we have found,
> within its reach.

There is a place where we can find one another, living or dead, and this poetic reality Olson shared with Robert Duncan—which you don't find, however, by rejecting, ignoring, or treating negatively or inferior your "gettysburg." The progression of BOTH (whatever they are) will be different from the ends of either, whether in opposition or synthetically fused.

An earlier poem, "You, Hart Crane" of 1940, had opened with the line: "Space—shroud and swaddle—you wore." Some American, Melvillean space is differentiable if one has two, *many twos*—"makes each a navigator," another version says, and then "a bridge . . . / Span made act . . . Myth propelled." Its very title, "Birth's Obituary," demands the mind remember its antithetical entry, at once a space and a history. Key West, February 8th, ..1945:

> I better make clear what I mean about these two traditions. Whitman and Poe show the contrast more obviously. Today Pound and Williams. I mean no greater and lesser business. It merely has to do, say, with the object of attention.
>
> It seems to me the central fact of America to the writer is SPACE. It is geography, at bottom, one hell of a wide piece of land from the beginning. That made the first American story— exploration. And something else than a continent stretch of earth: seas on both sides . . .

And so on—all of which will soon be transformed into the cadenced prose of *Call Me Ishmael* (finished the day the bomb dropped):

> I take SPACE to be the central fact to man born in America, from Folsom cave to now. I spell it large because it comes large here. Large, and without mercy. It is geography at bottom, a hell

of wide land from the beginning. That made the first American story (Parkman's): exploration . . .

How hard Olson had fought throughout the war years to hold on/let go as against the alternative generalities of humanism vs. simple space may be seen in this Notebook entry from 1939 (already several years into Whitehead at that point):

> The struggle of Melville's life was the transition to the modern—and in the struggle he lost.

His passage was from geography to man. Today space is no longer exciting: we're told of astrophysics & airplanes—Auden & Exupery—but they are & every day increasingly so, man's enemies . . . . What is the barbarous is not forest, today, but air. Space. Space-ships . . . . No, geography & the air are formed together & they are both bad . . . . [Melville] had discovered space. But something else in him, which enabled him to introduce "the humanities" into *Moby Dick* knew that the thing to explore was no longer the face of the earth but the face of man.

This same Notebook contains his notes to *Moses and Monotheism*, where he learned the story of the brotherhood of sons against the father (and mother, for that matter) crucial to the writing of *Call Me Ishmael* six years later. Some of the titles he doodled in another Notebook just prior to publication included:

MY COUNTRY IS A WHITE WHALE

I TAKE SPACE

THE FACT OF MOBY DICK

THE SEA, ITS CREATURE AND A MAN NAMED AHAB

THE BOOK OF THE LAW OF THE BLOOD

CALL ME ALSO ISHMAEL

WHALE OFF

March, 1947, with help from Caresse Crosby and Pound (whom he had visited regularly at St. Elizabeth's throughout 1946), the book came out, happily not entitled any of the above. (June in Gloucester he meets with Alfred Mansfield Brooks, director of the Cape Ann Historical Society, and from their conversation comes the idea of *The Maximus Poems* . Summer out West, gets Donner party material etc. from the Bancroft, meets Carl Sauer and Duncan. Back in Washington, 1948, second Guggenheim, supports Claude Pepper for President at the Convention in July, is invited by Josef Albers to lecture at Black Mountain College, then returns one week every month replacing Edward Dahlberg—his mentor since their meeting in 1936 when Dahlberg was living in Rockport—until the following Spring.)

Interviewed at home in Gloucester (where he had resided since his closing of Black Mountain in 1957) in that last year of his life, 1969, thinking back on those first years at the College, he says:

> The city's no good anymore, so where should we go? . . . Go where you are boss . . . Isolate yourself! Go into holes . . . Like in 'The Kingfishers,' which I wrote just at the time I was at Black Mountain. That's the point of the kingfisher—he lays his eggs in holes dug in banks. I mean, lay some eggs, for god's sake! Be fecund! Students, be fecund! And I mean fecund on the earth, in the earth Societies don't stand except by having feet. Two.

"The Kingfishers," begun in Washington in February and March of 1949 and finished in July at Black Mountain, was actually part of a longer work entitled "Proteus" and "The First Proteid" (not included in the *Collected*). The god of Change helps to context this difficult political poem (beyond its obvious debt to Eliot) with its Heraclitean opening: "What does not change/is the will to change."

Dahlberg may have been right, writing to Olson in October that "people do not change," but Olson knew something did, and, in fact, had Norbert Wiener's book (*Cybernetics*, 1948) to prove that

> not accumulation but change, the feed-back proves, the feed-back is the law into the same river no man steps twice

And then the lines that conclude the section:

> between
> birth and the beginning of
> another fetid nest
> is change, presents
>
> no more than itself
> And the too strong grasping of it,
>
> when it is pressed together and condensed,
> loses it

This very thing you are

What had begun for him at age 22 as picking up a white feather was now at age 38 not only a matter of creating the fowl of heaven but somehow jibing building of its nest with the feedback loop in creation itself. He had by now, of course, the example of W. C. Williams before him, so it wasn't only from Melville (White Jacket as Grand Collage come alive as Moby Dick) he learned to treat patch-work not as simple accumulation but to pay attention to the form and direction of interactions, both with one another and their unknown sources (of change).

Just where some "Bad Thing," or death, would be there is "the beginning of / another fetid nest." There is otherwise a tendency to look away when confronted with the horror of "the whiteness / which covers all"—space as "shroud and swaddle"—the desensitization Pound said characterized survivors of the Great War, as Allen reminded us. If the means of intervention, even Ahab's, are denied, Ishmael's survival seems as fortuitous as the post-mortem effects, then deemed natural. The West is doomed and there is nothing to be done about it now.

Paradoxically, a poetic rather than philosophic bent—that he would "hunt among stones," literally—left Olson open to the charge of being cold. In May, 1950, he wrote and sent to Frances Motz (one of three significant women of his life, along with the mothers of his two children) "In Cold Hell, in Thicket" in defense and acknowledgment. Caught between birth (an only child) and "another fetid nest" (the abstract), he was wary, like an animal, of readings of him, even his own, that would have expectation (therefore judgment) of ardent human relations other than those "wire-led" by his will—as instance of Western Man—to change. His living space and very air had come to depend on that progression begun at the mind's recognition of the method Blake had once dubbed "infernal." Yet, "the world goes on just the same." An event of *peripeteia* in poetic reality is "only a metaphysical tragedy after all."

Henry Corbin, whose work Olson said he could read about *his* world in, lecturing in Tehran in 1974, had this to say about our situation:

> History has been accomplished. Its eschaton, its final term, has come to pass. What is called *eschatology* in the language of theology in order to designate the events of the end, has already caught up with us . . . .. History ought to have come to a stop. Unfortu-

nately, History has gone on, but it could continue only because it had already overtaken an eschatology which up to then had oriented it in giving it its direction. Deprived of this eschatology, since henceforth it has it behind it instead of having it before it, History can only be *disoriented*, seeking desperately for a direction it can no longer find. Continuing on past its eschatology, History, in losing its direction, has become mad . . .. There is now only a pseudo-eschatology, which makes a pseudo-mythology of the 'sense of history' weigh down on our consciousness (*The Concept of Comparative Philosophy*, Golgonooza, 1981).

"The Kingfishers" posed the question: "shall you uncover honey/where maggots are?" By 1954, in a poem written to Frances, "I Believe in You" (significantly, changed from "I Believe in One"), addressing her as "Woman" and "Demeter," poetic reality is now

>knowing
the King of Hell

>also has you.

Not only the Kore goes down, but Demeter as well; likewise, uncovered honey may be appropriated and distributed in such ways as to become what in three years Olson will call "the simulacrum" (*Time* magazine's use of Homer, in "Some Good News"): history, "continuing on past its eschatology," as Corbin put it twenty years later. The very mystery religion which has oriented the West's continuance for two millennia ends up deferring to pseudo-history ("the Fix," Jack Spicer called it) because it perpetuates a little longer the cover-up of the fact that the "Greatest Story" exists now strictly in the form of its material analogy. In *The Maximus Poems*, an Herodotean, Olson will bring back in Libyans, Egyptians, Phoenicians, Minoans, and men and women of Gondwanaland before history was, all those removed from their *muthologos* that so threatened Western chauvinism from the 6th century on. Philosophy, which began as travel/exploration (i.e., murder), in its exclusive interest in Logos, whether to hold on, as usual, or let go, as recently, in either case, bears no resemblance to the project of *The Maximus Poems*, recent attempts to make a connection notwithstanding. History's twin,[2] for Olson, was politics, as space to time (and as a Catholic it would have pained him to see both reduced to sign), that is, politics—as discourse. Speech, one's own, he had learned (over Dahlberg's strenuous objections), made it possible for poetry to "uncover honey" in a place so measured that the homogenized history Corbin says weighs upon our consciousness could not pull it down into some Lacanian lair "to save for later." Now or never became the battle cry of "Projective Verse."

A first version of the essay already written, on May 17, 1950, Olson writes to Frances:

> That production at bmc last summer turned out to be a teacher of me. I tried to join music & instrument to speech. And the upshot was, no. What I have gone on to do, is to make verse, and its projection self-contained [revision illegible]. When you have a copy of the summer issue of PNY, and have the chance to read the PRO verse in print,—well, I have the feeling that is only scratching the skin of it . . ..
>
> THE MORNING NEWS, strangely enuf, seems to project most—Creeley will publish it in his 1st no. (do not know the name of his MAG), and will review y&x. And—of course—I am scared i shall never write another! It is the craziest sort of feeling, this, of not being able to match the done! (I suppose this plane is the sex of writing art, the underpart, the nervousness because love is not born. One loves only form, and form only comes into existence when the thing is born. And the thing may lie around the bend of the next second. Yet, one does not know, until it is there, under hand . . ..

We're of course here in the first Maximus poem, "I, Maximus of Gloucester, to You." He then quotes to her the lines beginning:

> the thing may lie
> around the bend of the nest
> second, time slain, the bird! the bird

Down to:

>   played
> by ear

In the published version the lines are changed to:

> the thing you're after
> may lie around the bend
> of the nest (second, time slain, the bird! the bird!

And so on, again different from the first version, down to:

> be played by, said he, coldly, the
> ear!

The next page of the letter continues to quote the poem, and then the third and final page returns to direct address:

> I'm sure, Frances, that, despite troubles, these webs which spin, get spun across the space, the wild and at times intolerable space, are flowers of life, are facts to bow to . . .. Anyhow, I give you the deepest sort of recognition, speak out from hidden islands in the blood which, like jewels and miracles, you invoke. And I, as hard-boiled instrument, as metal hot from boiling water, tell you, he recognizes what is lance,
>
> > obeys
> > the dance . . ..

The opening of *The Maximus Poems* , which he then quotes to her, is pretty much as it now stands, except:

> who obeys
> the figures of
> this dance

will become:

> who obeys the figures of
> the present dance

I would attribute all these changes for the better to the correspondence with Robert Creeley now begun. Because Creeley was other, or "Outward," to use Olson's word, poetic reality was instantly objectified. They were, without meeting, by writing alone, of such the same mind (note the difference in almost all their self-correspondence, call it) that Olson could, as he said, looking back in May, 1969, "make that whole thing/ double." The nest, no longer fetid could now be "next," and "second" could also move into both cosmological process *and* poetic reality, all because Creeley had given him the confidence of "what yez can do with rhythms in an open form," as he reported to Frances in a letter on "La Chute." Creeley was just 24, which Olson didn't know, imagining him in his thirties. For these years they shared a written speech, more mental than oral, yet not dialectical, and, in their work on poem and story, realizing that an anacoluthonic discourse could create its own space and then move into it, they had, if sometimes "beat" (Herbert Huncke's term for the times), embarked upon, playing it "by ear," a non-Euclidean "human universe."

Within five years Olson's "universe" had expanded to include, among others, Edward Dorn, for whom he proposes "A Bibliography on America." For example, under "Person" ("What used to be called THE INDIVIDUAL"), he writes:

> recommend, for light reading: homer's odysseus (for odysseus as more interesting feller than hamlet or captain ahab); mister jung, like i say (except that he ain't free to write—hides his 'creative' mss in a safe ["Sermons to the Dead," possibly?]—he is the one religious i mean he is serious in his attention to the importance of life as it is solely of interest to us as it is human, like they say, of any of the new scientists of man . . ..

But, for Olson, the problem is, just because analytical psychology was made scientific rather than creative to assure survival, its subject is still sacrificed to Enlightenment boundaries. In a 1950 letter to Frances he calls Jung a "swiss soft pink hill of learnin" . . . whom,

> by the way, I met once, engaged, and left, convinced he was a nobody. it was, I think, in 1938, in Cambridge, and under ideal circumstances, for pal [Henty A.] Murray had set it up. What a pretentious bastard (as, so very many, almost all, so-called scholars have shown themselves to be, in my experience: that incredible laziness, of specialization: the simple fact is, that it is not true, that, because of the increase of knowledge, it is no longer possible, or necessary, that a man seek to master it all, all . . .. The truth is, and what is not seen, except by the very best, the very few, is, that what a man has to do today is to devise some other method to accomplish coverage of the whole field of knowledge. And it is not the least of the reasons why an old device of man (what, because it is true, is called feminine, because the feminine is, as yr source sd, clear on essence, as man is on form) has come back into business as against the rational.
>
> For example, Pistis-Sophia, & the whole front of the ion (the nt. Jung lets his anima-animus discussbase, actually, of his

system, the mandala only another old wisdom wrongly taken hold of by him) become a corruption (a corruption of the minds of people now, god damn it) because he rests it on a decadence of the original energy which perceived Sophia as ANIMA. I have just gone thru his sources, and discover that, it is the Hermetics of the Middle Ages on whom he rests his case.

Today, not only in the semiotic impulse (where no distinction is made between arbitrary and actual compacts), but in the archetypal revision of James Hillman as well, gods and angels are allowed back in only as sign of complex. Blaser, alone, among contemporaries knowing of the issues at stake—including the social ones most duplicitous (in the analogy) for appearing out-of-order to those who work—has resisted positivism. Without a way to "make that whole thing/double," as Olson found, then, under the cyclopic eye of a sham history, as Jean Baudrillard warns:

'YOU are the model!' 'YOU are the majority!' . . . 'YOU are news, you are the social, the event is you, you are involved, you can use your voice, etc' . . .. since you are always already on the other side.

Apollonius of Tyana and Cabeza de Vaca became Olson's heroes of the healing arts because they change, as did his own art and life, under the law of feedback thrust upon them anew moving across spaces as diverse as their inhabitation.

Coming across "Zeus, Honey" reading Jane Harrison on Asklepios, Olson explodes in a letter to Frances, July 13th:

Again the necessity, the absolute need, NOW, to restate, to make once more available, the importance of the DOUBLE, of the two-faced nature of things, throughout Nature, the ambiguity of reality, to restate it because all rational thot, the lie, has raised up the generations to think there is ONE, and thus the burdens of choice, when, in actuality, there are ONE PLUS, which is sufficiently dramatized in TWO, in the binary (I would now rewrite certain passages in THE KINGS!)

The attempt to determine "the poetics of such a situation," that is, what we know went on, the dream: the dream being/self-action with Whitehead's important corollary: that no event/is not penetrated, in intersection or collision with an eternal event," of "A Later Note on Letter #15" (*The Maximus Poems IV, V, VI*), may place Olson closer to H.D. than to Williams (who thought Olson's poem of man and city, like his own, should have been named Gloucester rather than Maximus) or Pound (who thought of person as mask rather than image). Any of them now are of course unimaginable.

Maximus of Tyre, like the other Phoenician on Olson's mind, Melkarth-Herakles, addresses his "last first people" with blood on its hands, who try to "keep things clean, / by campaigns" ("Some Good News"), from off-shore islands hidden in the blood. Congruent mapping here, that is, is from off-shore Tyre, where Maximus is, to the Gloucester shore, where Olson is (until Volume Three when they come together, as Tom Clark pointed out in his Memorial Lectures). To show there had been no break in the continuity—established by Victor Berard in 1894—Olson in a 1962 notation played with his opening lines as though to make his "epic" follow from the prophecy at the end of the *Odyssey*, but without success:

> offshore by islands
> I, Maximus, an oar an oar
> stuck up into the sky
> and into the earth through to hell,
>> address you
> you islands, of men & plants

Already, in 1960, glossing the original lines in his copy of *Origin* I, lance was "scalpel," dance was "labyrinth" and "churinga-act," etc. which projects the field of the *Maximus* well beyond a Phoenician *Odyssey* via Asia Minor into stone age ancestral pathways, so why the seeming concession to literary epic at this point? Melville's advance had also taken him out of the Vergil-Dante verticality into the "Pacific Man" of *Call Me Ishmael*, but perhaps in 1962 he was nervous that that oar of American sea power being planted in Viet Nam by a new president (JFK had been a 'C' student of his at John Winthrop House, he said) would mean both Mao's vision ("The light is in the east") and his own ("the kingfisher flew west") would end in the hands of new global village idiots who would then decide the fate of the earth, its men and plants. "Like right now," he was saying in Andrew Crozier's *Wivenhoe Park Review*, 1965, "poor Chinese poor WESTERN GOODS good ben-rus WRIST-WATCHES on RADICAL CHINESE WRISTS"

("The Vinland Map Review"), a yielding to market realities that in ten years would mean the loss of Pound's Chinese Character to the Roman alphabet. Japan, as the whole world knows by now, is at the center of post-Pequodic effects. Olson's fifties prediction, in a short unpublished essay, "About Space," sent to Frances, concerning "that newest rigidity" (after religion and science) "collectivism," and "what Asia will do to collectivism," surfaced instead in the shift of people from "the motor force of history" (Mao) to objects of pacification, which is a little like asking them to join the Donner party (Olson's control story of the 'West' ending in ice and cannibalism) rather than, at least, Peter Weir's *The Last Wave*.

De-territorialization or "de-ideologization" (Mikhail Gorbachev), either way, it is the same "Dromocratic" Revolution; as Olson wrote in the *Niagara Frontier Review*, 1963:

> That the time now for some time has been post-Aristotelian and that there was pre-Aristotelian condition of discourse, has now to include Plato and Socrates and to see the set of them as proposing to change society, conceivably the most conspicuous attempt to do so prior to the present, and we don't even know what it does mean to change society comparably to how they did engage to do it, so much of our own discourse is in fact theirs. Thus social change in the present is boringly social and unequally revolutionary to theirs ("Review of Eric A. Havelock's *Preface to Plato*").

His essay "About Space" had ended with an anecdote:

> It is told how Diogenes once threw a plucked rooster through the window of Plato's school and leaned in to say, 'Here, here's Plato's human being for you.' Space revises time-man with some of the same shock.

The affront to generalizing time-man of man-as-object of a double-attention is that at any "second" he may bend time to its own shorter feedback loop (like Lawrence's "Escaped Cock" found the end of his tether), likewise recognitive of bounded space measures, say, "for a few feet," as Olson found in Dogtown, both poem and place:

> I can even tell you
> where I run out; and you can find
> out. I lie here

so many feet up
from the end . . .
("at the boundary . . .," Maximus, IV, V, VI)

In his Lawrence letter of November 5, 1950 to Frances, Olson had
taken up the question of survival:

> Generalization, now, is as dead as peace is, as war, is. There is one
> requirement only (and it, curiously enough, carries in it, does it
> not, one of the very clues on which love (the concept of) exists.
> That requirement is, stay OPEN, at all costs, stay OPEN, in
> order to be IN.
>
> It's gone far beyond survival, personal survival or any kind. It is
> not negative, or is it any longer useful to take either anarchistic
> position (generally the Bohemian) or the nihilistic (generally, the
> intellectual, I mean the fine, high mind).
>
> It is become a question, like this: these are the bases on which to
> erect new civilization, these very apparent contradictions. (The
> truth is, all they contradict, is, what was, what we have known,
> not human possibility, which, as I think, is to be circumscribed
> only by that other reality, which includes the human.

The following February, after some delay (his mother had died in
Worcester on Christmas day), Olson arrived in the Yucatan to open
himself to the poetic reality that had survived that change in the atten-
tions that had allowed the jungle to leap in.

Postscript:

In October of 1969, his own attentions changed, like the "Maximus"
William Stevens, ship's carpenter, Olson disappeared from his island,
Gloucester, in a rented Plymouth Fury to begin a new life in "Man's
Field," Connecticut. It lasted only to Thanksgiving day, when he first
experienced the symptoms (on the side of his face, and neck which had
been operated on in 1963, following the Vancouver Poetry Confer-
ence, when he was diagnosed as having a "tubercular tumor") which
turned out to be cancer, by then involving the liver, "live-her," as he told
Robert Duncan in New York where he had been taken, as he thought,
for surgery. But, for those weeks in Connecticut prior to hospitaliza-
tion, he had been, as he wrote in a note to himself, "living on the earth

as though it were a planet." His students at the University report the theme of his seminar was twofold: "We've got to fall back into the world" and "We've got to fall back into the word" (Last Lectures).

The gift of Olson's final poetic teaching, reduced and simplified since "Proprioception," was that the secret hiding place inside our bodies we've all lived in from childhood already made us "2-sided beings"; thus every human being has the means to work directly with the reciprocity between word and world, however apparently contradictory or as removed from one's own hands as Plato's cave —or, as Olson once said, what happens when poets become writers.

Not learning, but applicableness.
                    Reenact.
                              What you yrself then do.

        I am an enemy of Mantras, Mandalas, & Symmetry
        I am a Tantrist—that The Word is a book
                    that life is a book
        Working at our beings as 2-sided
                              functioning as dipolarities
                                        not positive or negative
                                        or contraries
                                        or dialectical oppositions
                                                  (in the jargon)
        To wrench on one tit
                    twists the other
        To have both hands on the levers at the same time
                              & unscrew the works
        To create a torsion btwn the one side & the other
                              gets at the reciprocity
                              of the not-always-equal sides of force.
        You create a field (*Last Lectures,* p. 13).

"What we make natural, we destroy," Pascal said.

The quotations from Olson's Notebooks and Letters to Ms. Frances Boldereff-Phipps in the Charles Olson Archive are copyright Homer Babbidge Library, University of Connecticut.

OLSON: THE BOOK

". . .that life is a book." Last Lectures

to Harry Martin

SOME YEARS AGO, SPEAKING AT NEW COLLEGE, I had occasion to
make use of Carl Kerényi's distinction between *bios* and *zoé* life. In
Dionysos, he writes:

> A wide range of meaning is bound up with the Latin word *vita*
> and its Romance descendants, and with *life*, or German *Leben*
> and Scandinavian *liv* as well. In their everyday language the
> Greeks possessed two different words that have the same root as
> *vita* but present very different phonetic forms: *bios* and *zoé*. . ..

> The word *biologos* meant to the Greeks a mime who imitated the
> characteristic life of an individual and by his imitation made it
> appear still more characteristic. . ..

> A Greek definition of *zoé* is *chronos tou einai*, 'time of being,' but
> not in the sense of an empty time into which the living creature
> enters and in which it remains until it dies. No, this 'time of be-
> ing' is to be taken as a continuous being which is framed in a *bios*
> as long as this *bios* endures—then it is termed '*zoé* of *bios*'—or
> from which *bios* is removed like a part and assigned to one being
> or another. The part may be called '*bios* of *zoé* .'. ..

> Plotinus called *zoé* the 'time of the soul,' during which the soul in
> the course of its rebirths, moves on from one *bios* to another. . .. If I
> may employ an image for the relationship between them, which
> was formulated by language and not by philosophy, *zoé* is the
> thread upon which every individual *bios* is strung like a bead. . . . This
> experience differs from the sum of experiences that constitute the

> *bios*, the content of each individual man's written or unwritten biography. . ..
>
> Actually we experience *zoé*, life without attributes, whether we conduct such an exercise or not. It is our simplest, most intimate and self-evident experience.

This *zoé* is the familiar Charles said (quoting Heraclitus) from which we are estranged, the simplest thing we learn last, given the limits each of us is inside of, as he has Maximus continue to "twist" around the "bend" of this life existing "through itself," yet "more than I am." In the "withheld" Letter 27 he had laid out, in a resounding epistolary voice too inclusive of the "ear" of Volume One (the shift from "*zoé* of *bios*" to "*bios* of *zoé*" Kerényi speaks of), the distinguishing thing about (his) *zoé*-life: "There is no strict personal order". . . "a complex of occasions". . . "of spatial nature". . . "forever the geography". . . "Polis / is this." The poet *sees* the connection between his own *zoé*-life and geography, which is the purchase he had needed for Maximus to address the *bios*-life of the citizens of Gloucester, even "little Charley from over the Cut." In the congruent mapping of "spatial nature" he had found a way to express that which to Kerényi is inexpressible, the thing that watches you in your drunken *bios*-life, the intoxication of Merry as *Maximus IV V VI* opens.

The theoretical side of Olson's work will have to do with the search for a vocabulary for this "double-track," whose sense as a "construction" you need, he said, to live. He went to Whitehead, especially the last chapter of *Process and Reality* where he discovered the word "dipolar," as a way to get around the mental numbing common to all dual-formations that imply you must go to the "transfinite" to satisfy "indestructible" *zoé*-life (as Plotinus does). As Melvillean, Olson knew of the offering of the White Whale as against Transcendentalism (why he also then had to clear up the confusion with Naturalism). Maximus takes the next, and colder step, in Dogtown II: "ice is interesting / stone is interesting" etc. As poet, his words, the said thing ("what is said of what is said") are the solidities that best express our "time of being," as Kerényi calls *zoé*-life. If *bios*-life is the "frame," that is not to say that our "time of being" is shapeless, formless, or any more "empty" than space is (contrary even to Einstein).

The upshot is that the studies that will re-begin with the publication of this *Allegory of a Poet's Life* must know from the outset that that old exegetical word that Olson got from Keats is in place of the emptiness of a life "time," and does not mean, suggest, or imply simply speaking at another remove from "the sum of experiences," Kerényi's characterization of *bios*-life. "Experience is, no matter how real," as Olson writes Duncan (1955), "only a system of metaphor for the allegory." The allegory itself, which Keats calls "figurative" (like the Bible), is on a different "scale," to use Olson's word. Keats' "life of worth," like those gravitational waves that "can't be bent" because they "already are narrative" ("The Animate vs. the Mechanical"), is the "string" or yarn running through the otherwise empty holes in those "beads" of experience we all are in (illusory) isolation. We are thus involved not in self-allegory masked as a life time, but in a *zoé*-life allegory that is its own creation, flood, exodus, revelation (which Keats says Shakespeare's works are the "comments on") *apart from* the "system of metaphor" one's *bios*-life may provide.

The shift in emphasis from Gloucester to Dogtown in *Maximus IV V VI* is the poetic registration of this seeing of the difference between the old politic-self (whether Prufrock, Mauberley, or Paterson) and the buried life (not the unconscious) *out there* in the "text of perception" (Merleau-Ponty), why he can now keep coming back to "the geography of it." This is noticeably a hard thing to get straight, perhaps owing to our hatred of earth (worms, bugs, snakes etc.). It goes against readerly habit to receive "eternal life" under image to the geographic, which must always remain on the "mundane" side of things. *But it is not possible* to read Olson's work or now this Book without "cartographic" admissions that won't come easy, didn't to him, a Catholic, and maybe can only be secured with adjacent reference to his "teaching" side, as for example in Connecticut at the end, still "fumbling" for the right word to indicate how it is possible to regain "our simplest, most intimate and self-evident experience" of the world, he introduced the term "evagination" (or "eversion") to help students then (as now) "learning to put the inside outside" (*Charles Olson in Mansfield*), these *Last Lectures* are his last (other than "The Black Chrysanthemum") address of the question, and provide almost a preface to this "allegory" of the life, if one can get hold of a copy (Northeastern University Press, Boston). The whole project fails if the *allegoros* (the other speaking) is placed on "This Side" rather than the other, which Olson clearly states here is the "stone of my being" (*in time*—and this is not Heidegger either) that "fell out." The other theoretical text to get going would be *Proprioception* (in *Additional Prose*). Once "projection" is worked "out," as he says, you find the "universe flowing-in, inside," which of course is the "river" you've fallen back upon all along, not the unconscious, which isn't solid enough to keep things straight for two minutes.

Even the Book can throw you off. For example, (fractal) time in Olson is much more "elastic" than even the rubber band image would have it at the beginning (p. 4), and certainly far from the Nietzschean "eternal return" evoked. There is no need to move to a meta-language when the Annisquam will do fine, to begin. But since we learn from the poem that it "bumps into" the "Other River" (as in the Egyptian system where the Nile is continuation of Heaven Ocean, the Milky Way), perhaps the mind minds better under image to the Moebius Strip. This brings the literal and the anagogical into the "continuum" in which there is "no break," leaving the "allegorical" and "moral" in the middle (numerically two to three in the 14th century Dantean exegetical tradition where "belief is allegory" and the "moral is what you do," *Patrologia Latino*). Olson knew of this fourfold from alchemy (Maria the Prophet) and of course Henry Corbin's account of *ta'wil* (exegesis) in *Avicenna and the Visionary Recital*, though in his own "system" he preferred the three ("what you do"), *typos-topos-tropos* (cf. *Poetry and Truth*) or *phusis, noos,* and *theos* (literally his Wesleyan fraternity, Phi Nu Theta). "I am an enemy of Mantras, Mandalas, & Symmetry," he told his Connecticut students.

Invoking "dipolarities" as against "dialectical oppositions," his colorful (and accurate) way of putting it was: "The wrench on one tit / twists the other" (*Last Lectures*, p. 13), thus his emphasis on the literal (as the numeral) to get to anagogy ("where you go"). As he explained in a videotaped Gloucester Interview, a *direct relation* to the flow, to source (as the Egyptian Nut) would only be "sucking off the tit" of creation. In *ta'wil*, as practiced by Al'Arabi at the Black Stone, the point is to move leftward, counter-clockwise, against Nature's dextro, the "dull copernican sun" ("The K") his experience of an inner-solarity ("heat") had confirmed. Later he found further confirmation of the fourfold in Kerényi's essay on Samothrace, how the fourth and the one become numerically congruent through the tropological (moral) act of turning toward greatest disorder (now the gist of catastrophe theory). Olson's attempts to discover sufficient "impedimenta" to compel the spinning quaternity to reverse itself, *literally* learning to trust his own "slownesses" (as that loafer Walt before him), were long in place before he knew what he was doing or why he was doing it. "The spirit of man is always ahead of his ideas," he told his students (*Last Lectures*), that is, already going the other way over "the Bridge" to meet the Angel, whether this meeting occur in life or in death.

One reason Olson's poetic is difficult to grasp is that the "method" itself is such that through the practice of the static the static is freed ("my Island has taught me" will be the refrain in *Volume III*). These two projects seem as contradictory as politics and poetry, which is why he had to leave one for the other (only to come back, too late, 1965). There was no "next" but the "bending around" to compose "by the total refusal, out the other side of any fiction, out where there is only totality itself. . .what these pieces. . .these markings on sticks or faces themselves compose" ("Billy the Kid"): the cybernetics of totality, I call it, he had hit upon, 1950 [at the time I was in the Crippled Children's Home with polio also learning to stop running]. This is the lesson we still haven't grasped as a people, "that it is, in fact more herd (more cattle) than gun (than any one of us even if we can shoot)." So, when you pick up the Book at your bookstore (as I did at Talking Leaves), drop your gun.

II

O WAS AN EGYPTIAN EYE

". . .psychobiographical studies must give way to a figure of more generous stature—poet and augur, Man of Space." Tom Clark, *Charles Olson*, p. 97

BEFORE ADVANCING VERY FAR into any biography we are asking ourselves the old question of intent: from what point of view is the book written? Robert Martin writes:

> Lord David Cecil used to say that he finally judged the quality of a biography by whether it had prepared him for instant recognition of its subject if he were to walk into the room and begin talking.

Trying that out, consider that the subject

> tried on ideas as one might try on shoes in a shop, making an appallingly fragmented task for anyone who sets out to recreate his life. The number of his intellectual interests was enormous, their frontiers ill-defined, their staying power slight.

That his

> genius was for wholly disrupting the lives and expectations of most of those who came in close contact with him.

That is, his

> impact upon his contemporaries was as often physical as intellectual, and he burst upon them with the random energy of an incarnation of the Romantic spirit itself.

But also that

> indolence was as much a part of his makeup as his energy, and his wonderful talk was often a substitute for more demanding thinking and writing.

And, finally,

> fascination with his own image indicates the self-reflective and self-dramatizing element of his nature.

From such a composite would you recognize this as Coleridge? That's not quite fair, only one of the quotes (the one concerning his "genius") is drawn from the new Richard Holmes biography, *Coleridge: Early Visions* (Viking) reviewed by Robert Martin (NYRB, Dec. 6, 1990) from whom the others are drawn just to make a point: that biography is a genre like any other, David Cecil's criterion notwithstanding.

Martin says of Holmes:

> I suspect he may not endear himself to all contemporary Coleridge scholars and critics by moving so easily between Kant, marital difficulties, Lessing, shortage of money, Jacobinism, house hunting, empiricism, flirtation, radicalism, and opium eating. . .

On the contrary, I'd say that's just the sort of weave we want. Otherwise we've got marital difficulties, shortage of money, house hunting, flirtation etc. as the "life" and, therefore, curiously, also the "work." In fact, Martin's main criticism is that Holmes

> is sometimes tempted into too-easy statements linking elements of the poetry with events in Coleridge's life that he believes may have inspired them. . ..There can be no question of how deeply rooted his poetry was in his day-to-day life, but the road from experience to artifact is considerably more circuitous than Holmes often suggests.

Although Holmes indicates that "the problem of understanding crea-
tivity is a finally insoluble one," biography as a genre does suffer from
this lack of circuitousness. Not attempting to plumb the process is one
thing, thinking to make do without it is another. As John Wieners
once said, "if we start caring too much for the immediate, we lose the
condition. We start thinking what we have done and where we came
from. We actually forget what brought us together. And that's proof of
identity" ("The Use of the Unconscious in Writing," 1967, *MFS*, #4).
Identity is not a commonality of vicissitude, but something far more
deeply interfused, and even more so when the meeting has not the bar-
rier of death to cross. Maybe there's nothing wrong with flat-out saying
it, as when Lawrence died Aldous Huxley called him "a being, some-
how, of another order." Isn't that why anyone would involve himself in
such sweet, protracted labors, to keep the beloved being in the vision
of *another order*, "the homeland of our thoughts" (Merleau-Ponty), not
to find flaw that leads not even to catharsis because the analogy is more
with the human comedy in this genre that does its level best to feign
disinterest in difference? Ever since that job on Poe, Platonizing biogra-
phers, contemplating their subjects without risk (cf. Martha Nussbaum,
The Fragility of Goodness), have relished the fall of the mighty. Ameri-
cans, especially, love only the underdog. The arrogance (root is *rogo*)
of creativity doesn't stand a chance against the poor "perishing nature"
Blake called our "vegetable" life.

In his last letter to George Cumberland, just four months before he
died, Blake wrote:

> I have been very near the Gates of Death & have returned very
> weak & an Old Man feeble & tottering, but not in Spirit & Life,
> not in The Real Man The Imagination which Liveth for Ever. In
> that I am stronger & stronger as this Foolish Body decays.

As Keats intimates, and Frances Boldereff's Philip Guston letter to
Charles points out (p. 137), the "Real Man" is "rarely revealed in the
biography, but always 'given in the work.'" The eye is to be trained
on the "emanative" life, as, say, John Huston attempts in his portrait
of Freud (who, in maintaining the inapplicability of his work to the
"creative," entered the creative, as Robert Duncan observed). "Other-
wise," as Charles told Duncan, "we are involved in ourselves (which is
demonstrably not very interesting, no matter who" ("Against Wisdom
As Such"). This can get us into the Dorian Gray area if we conceive of

the realm of art and imagination as aesthetic rather than emanative. It is a delicate balance, the two "sides" or "halves" of the process. Obviously the biographer can err on either side, but it's usually the *bio*-side that becomes the thrust over the *zoé*. Works are commentary, as Keats says, if the life is "figurative" (appealing to the Bible, as Blake does, as the "great code of art"), not simply interestingly occasioned, as he bears witness to Byron's or Olson might to Hemingway's. In a sense, a biographer's job is to suspend disbelief and follow the defensive Wizard of Oz's orders: "Pay no attention to the man behind the curtain."

Like anyone, only more so, Olson is haunted by his "Spectre." Blake devised a system of analysis so as not to be "enslaved by another man's." The method of psychobiography (Rank) does not hold the subject accountable for trying out on himself other systems in vogue, in this case Olson's amateur Freudian-Jungian self-analysis. It has the same status as any other "document," and is itself open to rigorous scrutiny. An author's honest impulse toward psycho-sexual determinations, even if generalized beyond any particular use to him, must not be used against him—especially the Freudian drive set-up, which may be "biological" (and semiotic) but not physiological or "proprioceptive" to the "present dance" of the "organs" (Cf. Ishmael Reed's account in *Mumbo Jumbo*). Blake says one is in one's Spectre's power until one's "Humanity awake." That didn't happen to Olson until Lerma (see *Mayan Letters*, especially the break-through bus letter), 1951, his "best" time and the best chapter in the Book. If you open it sprang in the middle, as though to begin *in medias res*, you'll turn right to it, Chapter 15, "A Human Universe," and all the rest will open out, both ways, letting its beautiful final tag carry you: "and is there any end, to that energy?" (p. 202). By then Olson has seen that the pathways of energy are more "tribal" than hypothetical (the arbitrary Freudian libido-canalizations), making him hunger after his own kind (cf. the Omaha Indian story in "The Gate and the Center," where "signature" is identity). Kindred may take a lifetime to find, but once found, all other relations to self and other recede into the background of impossible change. It was Olson's recognition that "one makes many" that made a Black Mountain colleague say to him: "I'm not convinced you believe in the many" (p. 212).

Olson's "depth inheritance," as he called it, was finally *act*ual, though he may have been attracted to Pound's "pagany" or Lawrence's "blood" before he knew that, before he had met any of his own kind. Creeley's first acid trip gave him the startling information: "it's not my eye, it's my father"; I'd venture Olson's as just the reverse. As "I Maximus" has it, etymologically, "Polis is eyes." He had tapped into a ground too easily referred to as "karmic." This, then, is the basis of the "allegory." In my case, as Robert Duncan said, because of Blake, Charles had an "appointment." Likely [Duncan's] "theosophical" orientation prepared him to "know" this. That doesn't mean he could see (or needed to) what Keats calls the "Mystery" of what in the end Olson called their 25-year adventure. Biographically speaking, it is simply a matter of positing it, that our democratic vistas do not contract to duck-blind just to bag our bird (which would be like taking Miles' word for it in his portrayal of Charles Parker in *Miles*). The point of building the city, polis, as Blake's emanative Jerusalem, which he called "liberty among men," is not to make the citizenry equal in the sense of "interchangable," but "Equal, That Is, to the Real Itself." Stated thus, it looks the impossible dream, but taken methodologically it is rather one more token thrown up from the well of mind to steady itself in a time Olson called "cinematic." It is a dogma of the "will to change" rather than change itself, which only ever occurs, if at all, in the fullness of time anyway. As Charles wrote me in "The Lamp," "who in fact is any of us / to be there at all?" I regard this "time," as it is cast ahead in Blake, prophetically and not, strictly, allegory, as the Book prospects it, nor Dahlbergian "parable," as Olson has it (p. 176). It has gone up the smoke-hole for sure, but it will be awhile befalling us. Themis' call to action remains for a "future age," perhaps the next millennium, however much our impatient "prophets" would have us "LEAP onto / the LAND, the AQUARIAN TIME" ("Dogtown—II"), which has led to all sorts of New Age confusions. Only the words say explicitly that it is "not to come until" "one day the / Vertical American thing will / show." The libertarian politics of either of these "Giant Forms," Maximus or Albion, unlike those of Homer's aristocratic Odysseus, is that all, everyone, must get back, home. Why, for Olson, Ahab was END of the "individual" way, and for Lawrence, too, which means poetry will bumble along in this no man's land for some time to come before Ishmael's dream of fellowship comes true. In the meantime, we must remain on guard against any further utopianism, or George Bush's New World Order, because it is our own future energies that are being sacrificed to it. Itself to itself, as the Eddic Odin had it, which in the analogy is how Olson saw the "uroboros" of poetry.

One reason Blake and Olson wrote in code, other than domestic fears, was so "the words" could not be "stolen." A possible poetic project for our "sad interim" (Shakespeare's Sonnets) is to take back the words already out there from prior unprotected sources, to "cap" some of the gushers like Red Adair & Co. are doing in the Gulf. I call this action, as Charles did (from Yeats), "antithetical" (my usage came from Novalis), because it works both ways, as over there more diverse hands than the Pequod are finding each other in "touch," which is a beginning. But we have had many of those. How, then, to trick Them into one They can't stop: that would be the poetics of the situation, geopolitically (textually, Olson's conflation of Enyalion, the war god, with the Norse Tyr or Tys who, for the common good, lost his hand, but then, as a Maximus, got it back through the poetic agency of Keats' "earnest grasping").

III

THE BUFFALO YEARS AND THEREAFTER

> "It is not I,
> even if the life appeared
> biographical."
>
> *"Maximus of Gloucester"*

MOST RECENTLY, I HAD BEEN READING, for Harvey Brown, Alan Judd's *Ford Madox Ford* (London: Collins, 1990). After a seeming plethora of unbecoming portraits ala Hemingway's *Moveable Feast,* we now have a documented Ford one would believe closer to the almost lost original, the Ford Harvey read and loved. For me, that is the key to writing good biography, love. Not the love that is a sin against the Holy Ghost Lawrence spoke of in his essay on Hawthorne—"The doom of the Pearl. Who will write that Allegory?"—but the love that is the advocacy of another standing before you at the portals. "Men with no ghost to their name" (*Studies*, p. 102) necessarily leave the matter in the hands of spooks, as though these planetary inconspicuitors will ever speak in our behalf. Listen to Williams:

> I laugh to think of you wheezing in Heaven. Where is Heaven? But why do I ask that, since you showed the way? I don't care a damn for it other than for that better part lives beside me here so long as I live and remember you. Thank God you were not delicate, you let the world in and lied! damn it you lied grossly

sometimes. But it was all, I see now, a carelessness, the part of a man that is homeless here on earth.

("To Ford Madox Ford in Heaven")

If we misunderstand this point of lying, then we *will* remain homeless. Large souls, like Shakespeare, point the way, lay out for us the real crimes, betrayal the worst. Blake, too was incredulous that we turn each other over to the Law without Urizen even having to renew his offer, *for nothing*. At least Ahab saw what he was up against, tried to coerce them with Sultanism to simulate magically the unanimity before (or after) fracture, the image of human failure. At the climax of *Jerusalem*, Blake's figure of time and imagination, Los, "cried at his Anvil in the horrible darkness weeping":

> Go, tell them that the Worship of God is honouring his gifts
> In other men: & loving the greatest men best, each according
> To his Genius: which is the Holy Ghost in Man. . . (pl. 91).

Blake's conclusion, that "there is no other / God," will need to be taken to heart if the "other side" of Nietzschean history is to be realized before the whole earth is run out of catalog. As Lawrence said, "masterless" Americans have yet to summon energy to go beyond into the specific freedoms offered by "the Spirit of Place." A simple thing like dropping the s off Jefferson's "pursuits of happiness" has made us, as Sherwood Anderson said, "grotesques."

The creature that now stalks our dreams, I must say, is not My Charles Olson, *nor* the one I read. I can't yet pin-point how that came about. It may be in the choice of verbs? There is definitely some cross-purpose at work, as though, protectively, the very sentencing would make sure the Golem doesn't, as Lord Cecil would comfortably have it, "walk into the room and begin talking." Maybe by now we're all so "starved from the glories of egotism," the Hotspur characterization Olson gave Alice Longworth (Teddy Roosevelt's daughter) we allow it only of our Irish Kennedys (p. 46). But it takes more than charisma even "to create a personality in this world. . .to come into life, and make the potential real" (Olson quote, p. 55). To make a "life" the "elixer" must flow from vein to vein, or pulse to pulse, the Keats-test for basic reading comprehension. Otherwise, "the advantage" of being alive spills out and washes away the subject, so that, paradoxically, even the writer is left with only a pocket-mirror intervention. A dead horse is more likely to fall on one than a live one. For an Olson biographer, not to go to the "Place Where the Horse-Sacrificers Go" ("On History") means the sheer weight of the dead horse after a while can only foster resentment. By page 75 an edgy tone, more irritated than Scorpionic, has begun to creep in, as though disappointed by the apparent gap between the subject's own words and the estimate being ordered on the basis of mounting evidence against their credibility.

The risk of "assuming the 'illusion of self'" (p. 92) Olson was well aware of. Cast in bald alternatives, "cool or fool," as he jots them in a late Notebook, Charles' (Trophonian) comprehension won't allow him other than fool, if there is a choice? Important to get the story straight (in place of that exposed anatomy they now call the sub-text): Dahlberg thought Bellerophon, I'd say more Samson than even Actaion, though Maximus does set himself up to go to the dogs. It's easy to make the fool (of love) look foolish, just look in the mirror, as Williams did (behind locked doors). Olson, like Whitman, is more open, even sexually, not as guarded as Pound. Modern crime is largely theoretical. In Olson's "post-" one does "belong," which means we enter the realm of the "wrong" and not simply "error" (which Olson called "minor didacticism"), Pound's "fascism," say. If Olson pulled the temple down on his head it is because he had the strength to do it. Lawrence had alerted him to the "high temptation of the mind," so he wasn't going down on that one alone.

As in Kerényi's zoé-life, the work would "occupy my days so that each to each is a bead strung on a steady spring" (p. 97). There are many correlatives to that steadiness in the Book, even in the preponderate wake of a previsaged "sum of experiences," like the long sentence beginning at the bottom of page 101. But not enough of "the planes of experience coming in from the past—coming up from the ground" (p. 143) are being simultaneously established. Equally Frances' "unworld brought to view" (p. 148) is not established early as poetic project, as against the worldly "personality as a pill of force" (p. 158) that, methodologically, held no interest for either of them. Next page, a "Lake Van measure" as unit only looks "bizarre" if the "holes" in the "nest" are not seen to correlate with a parallel search for "feathers" (to render "iron"). Thus you get (following page) a formulation like: "Cooking up a myth of neo-archaic man to fit the present had become an obsessive preoccupation for him," which loses the reader "myth," the "archaic," the "present," the "obsession," the "preoccupation," and "him," because the "beads" are strung on no real "thread." "The Mental Traveller," mentioned on page 166 as the Blake poem "sacred" to Frances (and Yeats before her), is more of a double-helix than the (unspecial) "cyclic view of history" here attributed to Olson, and in contradiction to the Book's own bio-weave in its treatment of "In Cold Hell, in Thicket" (p. 168), which reading illumines the otherwise abstract Tibetan "cold hell" Olson found in Waddell, though it isn't strictly "figurative" in Keats' usage. Nor is the term "allegory" used strictly, and is often replaced by "fable," "parable," "myth," etc. Charles' point about our being "guerrillas" (p. 187) is lost again to our "conditioning" as these pre-Renaissance matters (even "romance," as Hawthorne called his "allegories") lose their distinction within "the 'worn-out frame' of American culture" (p. 190). In "The Escaped Cock" Olson was prospective of the "guerrilla" love of the Sixties: "Its size and power increase again, and innocence emerges with a thrust much more than sensuality ever gave" (p. 246). These many years later we may forget what still sustains us in the attempt to overcome what Mike Rumaker calls here the "underlying or hidden malevolences" of the Fifties (p. 249).

After 1960, the Book sees the "quest" making "a religious poet of him," but as in the case of its exegetic looseness we are now confronted with "spiritual" categories as interchangeable, i.e., "semimystical," "shamanic," "hermetic" (p. 282) etc. Outside the "archaic" context of primary substances such terms have metaphoric status only, which is why Olson's poetics is at pains to find the means (in discourse) to overcome the episteme that lost it to us. Every major poet since Blake has discharged that assignment (which the lesser ones dodge) in one way or the other. From Olson's perspective, as the Book points out, Yeats fell on just this point (while his "secretary" did not). Pound never lost his "gyres" to the way his "finger smelt" however endearing that might be, an old man upon a stick is so relieving to most. Who needs (to backtrack to p. 258) "The Androgynes, / the Fathers behind the father," the giants Albion and Maximus, when you can knock down (prop up) the fantasy heterofather? Once the "archaic condition" holds you can lighten up, as Olson does when he calls himself "the Memphite lord of / Creation" (p. 283), a tonal register the Book doesn't obey.

Some corrections: p. 282, "Vedic" should read "Eddic." Norman O.
Brown was not then a "pop psychologist" (p. 289), but a classicist
(*Hermes the Thief*, 1947). His monumental revision of Freud, *Life
Against Death*, came out from Wesleyan in 1959, it's true, but he didn't
reach "pop" status until well into the next decade. Buffalo, 1963, the
Clevelanders Charles Boer and Charles Doria are also classicists (and
Audit editors with Betty Cohen), not "angeloi" in Stephen Rodefer's
metaphoric usage of a term of Olson's teaching. Adding the other
Cleveland editors of the first *Niagara Frontier Review,* Charles Brover
and Henry Lesnick (students of mine at Western Reserve), and others
of that first year at Buffalo, doesn't make a "reverent band of acolytes"
(p. 306). Al Cook is remembering the 1964-batch as "enraptured and
oblivious" more than this first one which certainly wasn't in a state of
"uncritical awe" (p. 307) when I arrived from Illinois. If anything, they
were skeptical, but loved Charles. The candy-eating incident (those
French bonbon fruits that come in a metal container with the noisy lid)
also happened the following year. The lady ejected was a faculty wife,
who then heard the "lecture" from the hall. The "one brown eye, one
blue" story (p. 306) has a follow-up, as I heard it. Linda Reinfeld, the
graduate student in question (I knew her in the late Seventies, now liv-
ing in Rochester), reported that when her mother sometime later paid
her a visit, spotting The Maximus on a table, said, "You know, I used
to know a Charles Olson in Worcester. We used to do our homework
together." So there may have been a deeper layer to this than one gets
from this telling. Artaud recommends that you "recollect your root
life within and against the Unconscious." By now Charles was getting
pretty good at it. The Onetto's-run here, and my quote on "those few"
(p. 307), also pertains to 1964-5 not 1963-4. The control word in my
sentence is "engage" (at Onetto's it was John Wieners, Harvey and my-
self), which doesn't mean Charles was any less gregarious or convivial.
Nor is "private faith" the best way to describe what we had that year
as a company (family). George Butterick, Al Glover, Fred and Pauline
Wah, Ruth Fox et al. were married and had their own lives and think-
ing; Bobby Hogg and Andrew Crozier never dropped their jaws, etc.
Of course within the English Department we were the "Olsonites," no
doubt about it.

IV

MY PIECE

> "That the object be allowed or made to yield its meaning but not be despoiled. That is, not used simply for self-expression."
>
> – Michael Rumaker, "The Use of the Unconscious in Writing"

MOVING NOW TO CHAPTER 24 (1964-5), Harvey Brown came to Buffalo (from Philadelphia) in September and stayed the first eight weeks with Sue and me before getting married (to Polly Jones) and moving into an apartment nearby. He didn't have "his money" yet, but would the next year at age 28 (from his Grandfather's trust). Charles paid for all our weekly nights out. There were three spots in a row, the Tai Won (Bill's Chinese restaurant which moved out to Williamsville); another Bill's, not "Luncheonette" (p. 317), but Deli, which later burned to the ground; and Onetto's which got torn down to build a Burger King. The University Manor Motel remains.

With "The Conventual" (Chapter 25) we enter an area of more serious qualification. To make a liminal category (see "Maximus of Gloucester," *Volume Three* and *Pleistocene Man*) read as "that isolated condition of subjective innervation which he thought of as 'the conventual'" (p. 327) is what Olson termed "biomorphism," or in his paraphrase of Jung, losing the *mystica* in the *psychica* (Jung was concerned with losing the *psychica* to the *physica*). This kind of psychological leverage (which Robin Blaser would call a "positivism") only perpetuates our failure to "get the Earth in," which Olson saw as an ethical dilemma. "Subjective innervation" as the "conventual" is a variation of the problematics of "allegorizing" in the previous chapter, where the "Love Generation" (p. 324) is equated to "the whole terrestrial angel vision." This "exciting cultural moment" was concurrent with "his world" he was "reading about" in Corbin's *Avicenna* but not its referent (see *Causal Mythology*). It does no dishonor to this time (which he also calls "acculturated") to differentiate it from actions discoverable only by and in another "clime." When Charles called to ask me about the surgery I'd had upon return from my Easter visit to Gloucester, 1969, I glibly quoted him, saying it (a melanoma) had been "lopped off the left shoulder." His stern reprimand was: "Never use your mythology negatively." That is, don't confuse it with your self, your life etc., keep it in the realm of *its own action*. I don't see the post-Berkeley Poetry Reading Olson as "confused." Not in Bristol fashion, still in the throes of mourning (itself a form), but by no means "only intermittently coherent" (p. 324). My friend Jean (Kaiser), for example, was then a student of Charles' in her own right, not just "acting out of consideration for what she imagined Betty would have wished" (p. 328). And though she might have come over to the Fort to help John Temple get on his way, John had held his own just fine with what by now the innocent reader must take to be THE MONSTER. The Olson Temple *confronted* (to Charles' delight) that first night after the Berkeley Poetry Conference at a big table in the back room of Onetto's was far from "nothing left. . .but the legend" (p. 328). By John's report *he also* had Charles "crawling across the floor" that night in Gloucester. Entering Charles' hospital room in New York, having driven up with John (from Mary Leary's family home in Oxford, New York where we'd been snowed in over Christmas), the first thing Charles wanted to know was where was John, "from way up North?"

Charles' other John, John Wieners, may have felt abandoned when Charles and Panna took off for England, but it was no "betrayal" (p. 332). He had already suffered the blow of being told he was "unfit to be a father" before Charles entered the picture as a rival (conception occurring at the University Manor not the Dennison House). At Cortland, where they met up upon his return, John's only accusation to Charles was: "You lost my scarf." News of the so-called "ménage" (p. 330), when received on the West Coast, perhaps got over-dramatized into a "double cross" (p. 337). When Charles broke into tears at the diner with Creeley over the fact "that the mountains can diminish and the seas dry up," that wasn't necessarily owing to "his current state of emotional turbulence" (p. 331) nor can I go along with Creeley's conjecture as reported here: "Olson had been speaking analogically of the diminution of his own powers, to him a process obviously of no less magnitude than the literal deterioration of the world." This is straight "pathetic fallacy" and loses the whole (out/in) point of the projective. Even without a literal / anagogy a poet's "affect" may engage the fact that

> "The sun will cloud over forever,
> the ocean dry up overnight,
> and the earth's axis crack"
> (David Rattray, "Rimas LXXXI," *Brief* 8, Nov. 1990).

The slim slip from life-metaphor to self-allegory elides the place of other speaking, which for Olson (and Keats) is the content under extension, never simply a way to "pretty it up" (O'Ryan). In this he differs from Williams, and even H.D. My Master's waters are nothing like "the Passaic." To return to Kerényi:

> And what does all this mean, save to realize the universal principle of life, the fate of everything mortal? What, then, is left over for the figure of Persephone? Beyond question, that which constitutes the structure of the living creature apart from this endlessly repeated drama of coming-to-be and passing-away, namely the *uniqueness* of the individual and its *enthralment* to non-being. Uniqueness and non-being understood not philosophically but envisaged corporeally in figures, or rather as these are envisaged in the formless, unsubstantial realm of Hades. There Persephone reigns, the eternally unique one who is no more (*Essays on a Science of Mythology*, 1949, pp. 123-4).

One of Olson's "capital" books, where he discovered the phrase "eternally unique," Kerényi helps offset the Freudian impression one may get from the "further testimony" (p. 345) of the "poet's absorption in the 'Oedipean' world tale he now made out at the heart of his self-allegory: the story of 'the eternally unique'. . . .." As an American born to "initiation" (*Causal Mythology*), Olson will go to "Eleusis" to "refish," as he said of Homer, the story, here in its "lesser mystery." But *it's the Kore* who is the "eternally unique," as Duncan said he had not seen her because he stood "in her way." A *yielding* to what is coming at you (in the *ta'wil*) is more in order than syntactically appropriating what has already happened. Self is entry, story end. Olson's objection to tragedy was that it stopped with death. With the Greek "Mysteries" he could go further (however, as he said, "dirty" the imagery), as Blake had found:

> The Door of Death I open found
> And the Worm Weaving in the Ground:
> Thou'rt my Mother from the Womb
> Wife, Sister, Daughter, to the Tomb,
> Weaving to Dreams the Sexual strife
> And weeping over the Web of Life
> ("For the Sexes: the Gates of Paradise").

It is she "who has died" (cf. Philip Dick, *Valis*), the soul/body, not the Self, which can never be "found." Nowadays we have family-therapy, where *all* are invited to participate, lest the one assuming the mantle of projection be gas-lighted, typically "the Big Baby." Otherwise, at the end of the chase, like those cops in L.A., no one knows quite what to do but beat you up. A Human Universe begins where the grip of transpersonal figuration leaves off. Without a life-allegory we are the automatons of a certain "freeze" in the action, collectively "castoffs," as Williams said in his great essay in behalf of Poe, "of another battle." Charles wanted to stop that battle, not just extricate *himself* from it, the lonely "psychological" agenda of this century yet to be entered. His radicality was "cosmological." He wanted to compel change in the collective psyche, not here but at its source. To go to "the end of the world," if need be, to deliver the present of what Reich called the "plague." It is no surprise that one who would do this would, like Oedipus, be blind-sided by the forces (now called "Oedipal") that don't want to be *seen* for what they are, spectral simulations of once proud poetic realities, and thereby replaced. If we don't complete this job, the union of the "proposed," to use Olson's word, with the factual half, the equally enormous one befallen him (us) under interpretation (because it's *there*, albeit, like any picture based on "digs," spotty), then we will have missed another chance with one of the "Lords of Life," as Lawrence says was his mistake once. It's too easy to side against Ahab, as we all have done (including Olson), without knowing the "greater" part of the "book" which is so outrageous, and brought so much down upon his head (and Melville's), it could only be "hinted at." The "Sea-Marke" precedes the Con(fidence) Man, but no one would go near it (which we must) were it not for the "masquerade." It's not that we must repeat it ("*imitatio* nobody," "Berkeley Poetry Reading"), but that we go close enough to notice our Whale is different from those stalked for their oil. This is the landspout that has "put all the diapers / up in trees" ("Tyrian Businesses"). Not Charles, himself, but the voice he left us in the middle of. As John Wieners wrote at the Plaza:

> I could not believe he would die
> even though my dream had come true
> and he had fulfilled so many
> ("Charles' Death").

For the record: the "temporary housekeeper" (p.341) was Ronnie Goldfarb, and the "latest live-in helper" (p. 346), Linda Parker. The "white linen suit" from Rome was actually off-white, and to "distinguish the garment from the man," as Blake says we must, and show there is no "gun" ("La Preface"), I must say that I do concur in the last sentence, it *was* a "long precipitate rush."

P.S. A tip to Olson biographers: note the two statements, both from Bill Levy's letters on Pound in the latest *Exquisite Corpse* (Vol. 9 Nos. 1-4, January—April 1991, p. 25):

> 1) "Most authors are content to signify the structure of self, or the spirit of a time or place. Like it or not, Pound always presents a complete worldview well-expressed."

> 2) "A man's work is honored in two ways. By preserving it and by carrying it on."

P.S.S. Since this writing I have come upon two more clues. The first from Jean Baudrillard's *Seduction* (St. Martin's, 1990): "They do not understand that *seduction represents mastery over the symbolic universe, while power represents only mastery of the real universe*. The sovereignty of seduction is incommensurable with the possession of political or sexual power." And the other from recently filed court papers which refer to the "Swedish Mentality Syndrome." According to Professor Ake Daun of the University of Stockholm: "Swedes appear relatively incompetent when it comes to arguing strongly and fighting back when attacked."

NOTES:

[1] Cf. Martin Bernal's trilogy, *Black Athena,* the first volume of which, "The Fabrication of Ancient Greece," is available from Rutgers U.P., 1987.

[2] Cf. W.V. Spanos, *Repetitions*, LSUP, 1987.

[3] for the speech-space relation, cf. *Hermes* by Michel Serres, Johns Hopkins UP, 1982, mentioned by Robin Blaser in his own Charles Olson Memorial Lecture.

[4] *Simulations*, Semiotext(e), 1983.

[5] *A Guide to the Maximus Poems*, p. 27.

[6] *Guide*, pp. 10-11.

[7] Cf. G.R. Levy, *The Gate of Horn*.

[8] Australian, 1977.

[9] Cf. Paul Virilio, *Speed and Politics*, Semiotext(e), 1986.

[10] Cf. Luce Irigaray, *Speculum*, Cornell U. P., 1985.

TRAMPING THE BULRUSHES

"It is an easy job to say that an elephant, however good, is not a good wart-hog; for most criticism comes to that."

"A clean Catholic will jump straight off when the time comes, if it does."

—Ford Maddox Ford

"Surely we are not psychological . . . the system which intervenes between a man and his path, and which intervened, historically, the moment when the secular overtook what wasn't, in the first place, 'religious,' in fact, when movement and thought (language as one) were split."

—Charles Olson, "Notes on Language and Theater" in *Human Universe and Other Essays*

"'Human Is' is my credo. May it be yours."

—Philip K. Dick

"'What was he, what was his trade, what did he do?'

'Nothing, he had no trade ...went thus from town to town and sang to everybody.'"

—Milman Parry

"Putting aside epic exaggeration, we may conclude that a song ["In the poet's mind the sequence of themes is the song."] may be as long as 2,669 lines, the work of a master who can keep his audience up all night."

—Barry Powell

"Yet Athena allowed the haughty suitors not altogether yet to cease from biting scorn. She wished more pain to pierce the heart of Laertes's son, Odysseus."

—*Odyssey*, 20

"Peoples who have reached this point of premeditated malice, when they receive this last remedy of providence and are thereby stunned and brutalized, are sensible no longer of comforts, delicacies, pleasures, and pomp."

—Vico, *The New Science*

"To conserve, to develop, to bring together, to make significant for the present what the past holds, without dilution or any deleting, but rather by understanding and transubstantiating the material, this is the function of genuine myth, neither pedantic nor popularizing, not indifferent to scholarship, nor antiquarian, but saying always: 'of these thou hast given me have I lost none.'"

—David Jones, "The Myth of Arthur"

"Capital ...is a challenge to society and should be responded to as such."

—Jean Baudrillard

"Christ, the bastards haven't even sense enough to stay out in the rain—"

—William Carlos Williams

"If a man or woman does not live in the thought that he or she is a history, he or she is not capable of himself or herself."

—Charles Olson, *A Special View of History*

"Spengler's prediction that the power to think will die out culminates in a taboo on thought which he attempts to justify on the basis of the inexorable course of history."

—Theodor Adorno

I N A TALK I GAVE ON OLSON, "The Metaphysics of Survival" in the company of Don Byrd and Susan Howe in Buffalo, I invoked D.H. Lawrence's poem "To Let Go Or To Hold On—?" in which he asks the question:

> Must we hold on?
> Or can we now let go?
> Or is it even possible we must do both?

To do *both*, as Charles Olson did, required an ordering of experience of the antithetical influx of our time, more than those, who now at century's end have more comfortably slid into a "let go" mode which by now must seem consensual, if not constitutional. Of the few still alive who methodically "hold on" whom one might turn to for inspiration, I might cite Robin Blaser because he can even give us a formula: scholarship—cosmos—happiness. Even faulty scholarship, as we know from Sun Ra, can "work." Olson, usually a stickler, could go off the deep end (as Pound did), for example, with L. A. Waddell and still come out in the "right" place: "The whole question & continuing struggle to remain civilized Sumer documented in and out" ("The Gate and the Center," *Human Universe.*)

Knowledge (which is at issue here) based on scholarship is of course self-correcting. When Olson learned (from Spengler) that in declining civilizations knowledge goes to the edges, the new frontiers, rather than remaining central (why the CIA can no longer keep up), because he *could* "let go" in order to "hold on" (and this is his advance on Pound), he could cast his lot with Ed Sanders' "ZD Generation" (after Zola and the encyclopedist Diderot); today he might be with hip-hop at the Giant Step? Such a stance is easy to mock. All you need do is, as Ed would say, "zombie" this "whole question & continuing struggle to remain civilized," as though it were a "right" susceptible of legislation like most else today, something you walk on, like the street, etc.

To Disch, Olson's learning to tramp the bulrushes in which God does mysteriously work, makes him a "beatnik guru" (another near oxymoron like his "iambic megalomania"), a "high priest [the title Tim Leary had given his own 1968 account] of high times," whose "knack for creating disciples" is what made for him a "special place in the history of postwar American literature." If anyone is a "disciple" I am, and can assure Disch (he may even remember me, as we shot pool together with Harlan Ellison after he had bowled with Cass when she did PR for "Just Buffalo" [1980]), I have no pull with any canonizing powers. And if we start with Black Mountain rather than Buffalo, where the pejoration is deflected (while retaining the religious metaphor) to "acolytes," we won't find anyone there either who somehow carried Olson into the limelight. Even notable *peers,* Robert Duncan, Robert Creeley, Denise Levertov, Allen Ginsberg, Michael McClure, et al., have had no greater leverage in bringing Olson into their company; anymore than the indicated macho "tastemakers," James Dickey, Robert Bly et al. could bring him down. If Disch wants to invoke a "heavy" saying "weedy and colorless" (Marianne Moore), why not be fair and quote another, W.C. Williams saying *The Maximus Poems* "staggered" him, calling Olson a "major poet" (and including the "Projective Verse" essay in his *Autobiography* because it spoke to the advances he knew to have occurred in his—for the first time non-metaphoric—field?) In the end, Disch abandons the flunky argument; using terms like "self-anointed" (which must be like Napoleon crowning himself), "megalomania"and "mad," rather indicating he thinks he's onto a case of (that most typical of) delusions to account for Olson's problem: hunger for sycophants and too much booze and drugs. We know exactly who those are who fell to those things. We can name them, and Olson would not make the list. More than anything, his hunger was for history-as-inquiry (etymologically, "to find out for yourself "), as the "new localism," not this de-molition-by-proxy (as Thoreau pointed out) which now "they say" (words Williams' Aaron Burr cautions us never to use) is at an end; which is the "frame" of mind we're in ("quiet desperation") without cosmos: not a question of holding on or letting go, but of Them vs. Us, a diminishment.

For Robin's formula—scholarship—happiness—really to work there is an ingredient to be added, which I'll give you. Or, let's say, the secret and the challenge, which is the last word I heard Charles say at his deathbed (cf. the first poem in *Fathar* III, if you have a copy of that first collection of mine around). Jean Baudrillard writes:

The hidden or the repressed has a tendency to manifest itself, whereas the secret does not do so at all. It is an introductory and implosive form: we enter it, but are unable to exit. The secret is never revealed, never communicated, never even 'secreted.' It derives its strength from this allusive and ritual power of exchange (*Selected Writings*, Stanford, 1988, p. 159).

In what Baudrillard and Henry Corbin both call "the secret of the secret" there is no "hidden information," for, "everything that can be revealed lies outside the secret." It is not "the key to something," Baudrillard says, "it circulates through and traverses everything that can be said," and *fast*. The problem, as you might expect Baudrillard to intuit, is that the secret can be simulated:

The 'adventure' of the unconscious appears to be the last ambitious attempt to fabricate secrets in a society without secrets. The unconscious would then be our secret, our mystery in a confessional and transparent society. But it really isn't a secret, for it is merely psychological.

Since he also speaks of "the joy of secrecy," perhaps for Robin the formula already contains the secret in happiness, or Coleridge's word he often prefers, "joyance" (cf. also "Apollonius of Tyana," *Human Universe*, Grove, 1967, p. 41).

"Why do we answer a challenge?" Baudrillard says because of "a mutual vertigo" of "absence that unites," again the secret, now determinedly rhythmic (i.e., you had to be there). What you cannot have is a secret contract, the final oxymoron behind all these attempts to shore up the simulation of knowledge-culture. The challenge of Olson (what challenged him), like a secret, "is immediate, immanent, and inevitable." The "transcendental" paradigms will always fail to account for "enchantment" which Baudrillard says "puts an end to every libidinal economy, every sexual and psychological contract, substituting in its place a staggering openness of possible responses. It is never an investment but a risk." The risk of openness to the antithetical which, like Olson's "Gold Machine," is always operatively BOTH a holding on AND a letting go. Novalis said that mutual propositions are strengthening. That's exactly how it was being with Charles Far from the mono-line, as Baudrillard says: "the challenge consists in driving the other within your area of strength, which is also his or her strength, given that there can be an unlimited escalations (cf. again "Apollonius of Tyana," p.35). For us it was Melville and Blake, but for anyone it was something, and *if one didn't yet know what*, Charles *did*, and spoke to you *as though* you did know, a generosity I've seen in no other save a mother, a relation no one would call discipleship. The way out of unhappiness may come but once in a lifetime. Is having missed out on it the reasons of *resentment* (remember, also Nietzsche's word)? A quick example.

Once, when Charles was relating to some nice old ladies and other neighbors in a small company out in Wyoming county his two mushroom experiences with Tim Leary (Dec., 1960; Feb., 1961), and at the end of the conversation, incidentally explaining to them how he's discovered the number of dependents he has to claim in order to get his full paycheck from the State of New York (incidentally, Charles was instrumental [always] in getting the administration to hand deliver all our paychecks), he has for the umpteenth time in his life (one week before They kill the president) to create enough space to retain the human province:

Voice : Perhaps these drugs would help with income tax problems.

Another Voice: You gonna take them, or feed them to the tax collector? [General laughter]

Olson : There we are, right back at the whole problem. Leary wants to feed 'em to Khruschcev and Kennedy. I think that politics stinks, myself.

Voice: What does Dr. Leary feel would happen if this were used on a large scale?

Olson : Oh, he thinks happiness would descend upon the earth [laughs] . . . And he's right, you know. He's talking euphoria.

Voice : Well, what is happiness?

Olson : It's the state of confidence that you're alive and in life [Others join in laughter over defining the terms of 'happiness'].

That's from George Butterick's transcription of the Gratwick Tape ("Under the Mushroom," *Muthologos*, vol. 1, Four Seasons, 1978). My point was to show the mutuality of the process of discovery, how happiness itself is found to be found, to everyone's relief, definable. Our pursuits, as Jefferson called them, are knowledges, knowledge-bringing-events (Merleau-Ponty) which, phenomenologically, constitute the world; what Robin calls cosmos, thereby happiness, its secret and its challenge. The tape breaks off with Olson telling the group of a "wonderful bibliography. . . ." Drugs were clearly not his road to Xanadu.

Let me pause to offer a personal anecdote. In the Winter of 1964- 5 Gary Snyder had come to town—it must have been just prior to Christmas break (waiting with Charles at Onetto's for Gary to arrive I remember Charles saying "Santa Claus is a true god")—later in the car, Charles at the wheel, Gary had passed me titles of five scholarly Buddhist texts from the back seat and had written each one on the back of the notebook I was using for Charles' mythology seminar. Weeks go by and Charles says to me: "I got four of those titles, but what was that fifth one Gary gave you?" I looked at my notebook. "You see, that's the advantage of writing," he said. I, on the other hand, not only hadn't remembered any of the titles, but hadn't acted on the tips (still haven't). Whether he had or not, I know the transmission was treated as a serious one not only because *he* had heard it but because it took place in a "cosmos" of hearing. This is not witchcraft (Adorno), it is what's possible when one learns to use oneself coincidentally with the "rhythm" Baudrillard speaks of (we know primarily from the control Novalis quote Olson circulated). Anyone willing to take the risk of openness quickly notices the difference between a phenomenological statement like "Equal, That Is, to the Real Itself " and what Disch here takes to be the rhythm—between "sloth" and "manic bursts of overexcited, under-developed brain-storming" (not to mention that as a writer he would not also recognize this "pattern"). The author of seven volumes of verse (including *ABCDEFG HIJKLM NOPQRST UVWXRZ*, 1981), unac-countably Disch loses any credibility he might have had when he simply loses it to: "Olson scarcely did a lick of work, except to write poetry and prose. . . " Jesus, call the police, send in the FBI ("Look! he stut-ters!"); then, when the writer who said poets should "getta job" gets one "teaching" (note the quotes) Disch says that don't count, for it was "in the filibustering manner of a barroom philosopher." Certainly a perverse sense of stamina. As more reports from actual students roll in over the years such distortion will seem laughable, now it's not so funny. It's even dangerous, *given* the present struggle ("to remain civilized"), tenuous enough in this age of Material Analogy where "unlimited escalation," as Henry Adams foresaw the Spectacle, ends in cybersteroid mutation.

In his genre of competence, fiction (he has a new novel, *The M.D.: A Horror Story*, from Knopf), primarily Sci-Fi, Disch doesn't seem to see one of its masters, Philip K. Dick, whom he knew, any more clearly (or fairly) than he does Olson. In his biography, (*Divine Invasions: A Life of Philip K Dick*, Harmony Books, 1989), Lawrence Sutin quotes Disch's account of their September, 1974 meeting:

> I thought: Interesting—a masterful con that works. He's a profes-sional entertainer of beliefs—in other words, a con man. He wants to turn anything he imagines into a system.

This again invokes the image of the "barroom philosopher" (Sutin says, "Their talk, fueled by beer, went on for twelve hours. At stake, it seemed, was Phil's probity.") or the pejorative "autodidact" he uses on Olson, rather than the real man of knowledge (and learning) Dick was, which Disch sees in the extreme as "delusions of reference." I can't say, but I do know his charge that Olson at Black Mountain "was a pioneer in the dismantling of the college core curriculum and its replacement by a kind of autodidacticism that differed little from autointoxication" is unfounded. In fact, just the reverse is true. Olson fought for the core curriculum of the school's founder against a less rigorous "arts-and-crafts" contingent (see *OLSON* 2, Fall, 1974, "Statement for Black Mountain Catalogue, 1952" and "A Draft of a Plan for the College, 1956"). From the beginning, as John Andrew Rice stated it in Black Mountain College *Bulletin* No. 1, November, 1933:

Dramatics, Music and the Fine Arts, which often exist precariously on the fringes of the curriculum, are regarded as an integral part of the life of the College and of importance equal to that of the subjects that usually occupy the center of the curriculum.

And in his autobiography, (dedicated to Louis Adamic), *I Came Out of the Eighteenth Century* (Harper, 1942), Rice states, in terms reminiscent of Blake:

The center of the curriculum, we said, would be art. The democratic man, we said, must be an artist. The integrity, we said, of the democratic man was the integrity of the artist, an integrity of relationship.

The tradition of the autodidact (from Vico to Harry Partch) needs, of course, no apology. And, many have been equally capable of the marathon monologue (Duncan, Creeley, Stan Brakhage . . .). The appellation "barroom philosopher" is better suited to Ralph "Bottles" Capone, "Big" Al's older brother, whose bar was "Billy's" in Mercer, Wisconsin. I doubt that "Bottles" was attempting a system or a cosmos, though he is reputed to have been a sweet and generous guy whose widow still lives there. Maybe she should be sounded, just to break the ironizing pall we *all* may cast. I hope Frances (Boldereff of the Book) won't mind if I tell you what she wrote to me in a letter (July 14 [1991]): after Charles died Connie came "to sit beside me in my living room—I had never seen her nor communicated with her—said I was the only person who would understand." I say this in lieu of commenting on Disch's portrayal of the women of Olson's life, and their relationships. It's not repeatable. What would he do, I wonder, with Ford's life, where there are *eighteen* women "including one of considerable importance of whom nothing is known except her first name, which was Elizabeth" (Ford's last wife, Janice Biala in Alan Judd, *Ford Madox Ford*, Collins, 1990).

I also don't need to comment on Disch's picture of Charles' descent from "his moral nadir" by the end of Black Mountain to "tenured professor (actually he refused tenure) in the academic equivalent of

Skid Row." Al Cook has answered that in a letter to the *L.A. Sunday Times*. Al points out that we were rated in the top twenty when Charles was in the Department, "it might have been rated not just among the top twenty but one of the two or three very best—if not in fact then the very best of all." Tracking his movements from Harvard, Al knew what he was getting into hiring an egregious sponger and a tenacious uninvited guest, yet at Betty's death the Cooks were first to open their home [it was there that I first met Charles, at my own hiring party] to the Cyclopean poet who by then was certainly well into "his career as freeloader and professional guest." When I first saw him (he was 6'7" not 6'8") he was teaching their youngest son Jonathan that Uruk was the first city. Nor do I suppose Charles Boer would change even what he put up with when the two "Chollys" found themselves briefly under the same roof those nights of that final year (*Charles Olson in Connecticut*, Swallow Press, 1975)—Olson's best line (after having been thrown out so Boer could get some sleep!): "Never shove the one who loves you." In their reversed roles, father to baby boy: "I said I wouldn't," (p. 81).

This whole question of discipleship contains more than meets the eye, as we, who have lived under it know. Clayton Eshelman was more mollient, he called us "novices" (which I liked because of Novalis' *The Novices at Sais*). I'll get at it with another anecdote. After a lobster meal (which he had cooked) for a gathering of five at a faculty house, Don Barthelme put me in the position of having to defend Creeley's stories. He dismissed the poetry outright. When fiction writers regard poetry, as Disch said in the *Nation* (Nov. 27, 1989), among the "no-longer-living arts," nothing can be happening almost by definition (without looking). It couldn't come to blows (he already had a broken arm in a sling from a fall), but before he stomped out (the hosts having to follow by car unsuccessfully pleading with him to come back), he did point out to me sternly that if a man of my age was still defending another man's work I might as well forget it (any creative aspiration) because it was already too late. That if there was need at all of apprenticeship I had exceeded it (I was in my thirties), I took him to mean. Not to lay anything on Don, now that he's gone, but I do think that incident echoes some of the assumption behind the persistent rancor over Olson and his, well, he once used the word "gallants." You're simply supposed to abandon the conventional wisdom of, as my mother gave it to me in the adage, "Never toot your own horn," which those who actually do toot horns never do (of the lady trumpeter from L.A. he had just met in Russia, "I learned a lot from her," Dizzy Gillespie at 73). I hate to leave the question hanging there where Harold Bloom left it (*The Anxiety of Influence*, Oxford, 1973), because it's not really a matter of the implied "father-son" psychology, but much more in the area of risk and challenge, as Baudrillard has it.

On sabbatical in Oregon in 1970, I wrote a poem, "Mental War is Combat for the Angel" (again *Fathar* III) derivative mainly of Blake and Corbin, whose first lines tell what I took to be at issue twenty years ago:

> You fight your heart out objectively
> to win the battle each wound a stroke
> of love between opponents of like skill
> or rank or honor to find these pairings
> or doublets in which each can do death
> battle for the other otherwise unfair
> hence the three choices humiliation
> before the beloved apology to the enemy
> King Arthur's Court to be farther schooled
> unmistakable societal conduct and why
> we so need these structures The Forms
> of Experience . . .

I remember being excited finding the limit of three choices and their equal efficacy, the third perhaps the one to fall back upon except there wasn't one (as Yeats had pointed out). Now if I thought (and still do) that those who would befoul Olson so to bury him had truly (consciously) undergone either of the first two choices (Beulah and Eden to Blake)—whereas *actually* the only "public realm" (Hannah Arendt) of any remaining humanity is likely kids in school (Blake's Generation and Ulro)—would I, or Robin, or anyone of us, not have desired to be drawn up into that accomplishment rather than tarrying here (with Olson) to improvise (that art Adorno spurned) an Arthurian Camlann? The whole reason Americans have fallen into this simulation of Baudrillard's is for not being commensurate, not beginning where things really are. Now of course nobody gets it right the first time (cf. Pound's story of how Fordie saved him by rolling on the floor after hearing his "mehercule" poems). In a revolutionary period, as not only Blake but Wordsworth and Keats had showed, it is the stepwise advance from an *arrived at* beginning (as in the Olson formula, "All but heat is reductive") by which any work of further society is made. Barthelme, like anyone with his wits about him, started with "An Island in the Moon," and *took it from there*, whereas Blake saw there was nothing there to "build on" so turned this "Hell" into an "Infernal Method" and burned his way down (and out) to " Holy Thursday," the ever- diap e red "bottom" he named "Innocence." In the end, when you find Blake making those first two choices (in *Milton* and *Jerusalem*) you know they have come from a lifetime of back-tracking (unlike the manic locomotive also invented that year, 1804) to "Arthur"-(Albion)-educed beginnings, so are on (just as) solid ground (the coincidence of "youthful prime" and "golden clime"). Textually, it must be called "prophecy" because if one tries to opt for them in "real life" one inescapably enters the simulation. Whereas Disch calls Olson's life a "dishonest" one, Blake knows "deep dissimulation is the only defense an honest man has left" (Erin to the Daughters of Beulah, *Jerusalem*, pl. 48) in an age "in which all shall be pure & holy / In their Own Selfhoods." We all know by now where such *purity* leads. And you were right to call me, Steve Baraban, on my misappropriation of a line of "La Préface" in that Olson talk (*Acts* 10, p. 151): "born of those dead Hitler gassed," as you say. This is what is at stake (Adorno, again), has been since we neglected to notice, it happened so fast, where things have been at ever since (abridging Brooks Adams) the gold and silver mines of the new world helped to create an economic vortex in Europe finally to make mechanical (coke-iron- steam) application of the universalized version of Greek comparativism left from Baghdad. Hence Czeslaw Milosz's *The Land of Ulro* (Farrar, Straus and Giroux, 1981). I think what happened, as Fordie sported, is that the new situation was "ridden" (and then profitably overridden) by the "modern" instead of ever stopping to take stock of the situation. Olson was one of the last to dare intervention upon our time. He left a huge monkey wrench in the works and, I think, that's what is so resented by the Hierarchy. So when the game is done, who has won? Not to worry, Milosz says:

> Weathered by time, the transitory and the spurious fade into gray banality; but they may also lose their appeal when confronted by a more powerful beauty, one more abundant in *being* [excuse his Heidegger]. Works less abundant in being are put to death, not by critics or canonical pronouncements, but by works of greater

abundance. Which raises the question of whether a work kept in a drawer, or a painting condemned never to leave the artist's workshop, can be said to have the same power. In my view, they do—and this brings us, finally, to the law of magical intervention through unseen communion" (pp. 88-9).

There you have it, the secret, yours and mine, the Yugaic progression *from feathers to iron*, doesn't matter, even "unmitigated disaster." *Read the work!* "It is still / morning" ("Tyrian Businesses").

P.S. And so come across them talking elsewhere tonight (Sept. 26), though it is the Doctor's undersong, "The Descent," above the muffled words—bids me to live.

> Duncan: Oh, one thing that's on my mind right now is if you take that first stone as given, and under it or into it could be set 'this is She.' If you get to the Greek image, the one that Charles is talking about at Paphos, by that time 'This looks like Her.' As a matter of fact, between these two statements this looks like her, and she is someplace—she is an idea, and then she floats all over the place, she's beauty and she's anything they want to name. The thing you do know is that—as a matter of fact, when they dig her up they know—that's what first things are, that this is she, and she proves to be stone . . . You're always working in a poem in the same thing that man has worked in. And when you came to idea poets— and Shelley's certainly one of them, and it's beginning in Wordsworth in parts you are cooling to a separation again between the statement 'this is She' and 'This is like Her.'

> Olson: I think so, very much, because Wordsworth's weakness is not at all that he had a system of thought, but that nature had become a substitute for this thing that we're now talking about— like literally nature—you go out and you see. Or he gets scared by a looming shadow out on the boat on the lake [*The Prelude*, Book 1]. He ain't being scared by a looming shadow out on the lake on a boat. He's being scared by some funk in himself. And we know these things. One of our chances is to be sure that we could place the funk where it belongs and not distribute it as though we were dealing with formal character of the real.

P.P.S. Leaving, then, Vancouver, 1963, to enter *The Lost Dimension* (Semiotext(e), 1991) find Paul Virilio quoting Einstein on the (Rilkean) dare:

> With the invention of the electromagnetic field, a daring imagination was needed to fully comprehend that it was not the conduct of bodies but rather the conduct of something that existed between them, i.e. the field, that could be the essential for ordering and interpreting all events (p. 97).

NOTES

[1]. As instance (of many) cf. Dieter Lenzen, "Disappearing Adulthood: Childhood as Redemption": "that the world might 'become completely barbaric once more', i.e. that it might 'decay into childhood' (Fontenelle) has been explained time and again with increasing frequency over the past 150 years as the royal road to salvation" (*Looking Back on the End of the World*, Semiotext(e), Foreign Agents Series, 1989).

2. Cf. Hakim Bey: "the Wild Man is lodged like a virus in the very machine of Occult Imperialism" (T.A.Z, Autonomedia, 1991).

"ONE SIDE TURNS INTO THE OTHER EASILY"

[Jack Clarke carried out an extensive correspondence with Tom Clark while Clark was writing Charles Olson: The allegory of a poet's life. *Clarke initiated the exchange, which runs to some 200 typewritten pages, in hopes of influencing Clark's increasingly hostile relation with the subject of his biography. He was unsuccessful. This letter was written toward the end of the correspondence after the book was published and the first reviews using Clark's book to attack Olson began to appear.—MB]*

June 28 1991

Dear Tom

Like you, I'm losing strength over this, but wanted to give you the context, as I guess I must not have. Before they left town, Pen & Cass were on the phone, Pen said did we see the Disch dis, Cass said yes, Gerrit sent it, but did you see the Dawson letter, no sez Pen, Robert and Fee no longer speak; and so they agree he's an asshole etc., so when she tells me I take it to mean they want to see it, Fee's letter for the joke it is (as she said Bob's response to the Disch was laughter), which is why I sent it to them. Actually, there were three "unexplained" enclosures (mailed with intent.). Charlie Palau had tried to deliver by hand but Bob had already split for Me.) a fax from Bill Sylvester, which had been put in my box at the Dept. by mistake; a letter from a would-be subscriber who said he didn't want any intent. (pay for) which didn't have RC in it, which I thought Bob might get a laugh out of; and 3) the Dawson. There was no need to send Cook's response to Disch as he had already sent a copy to Creeley (Al said). None of these needed, I thought, explanation, so were simply stuck in, as Palau had returned them in the envelop, especially not Fee's effluvium, or as I take it Creeley thinks to call "filth," though I don't see why you call my sending it to him "second hand slime"? Nor do I see how 2 people getting it constitutes "circulation"? This construed question of the great UNEXPLAINED ENCLOSURE is a red herring anyway. (I'm sure Pen told him of the conversation so knew it was possibly coming.) Bob's piss-off, if that's what to call it, is from other reasons entirely, I'm sure. He has you know now withdrawn from the Curriculum (by letter to me and to Glover), so to him it is the end of 20 yrs. It all started of course with Duncan's failed Olson Memorials, which both Harvey and I cancelled, if again that's a word to use w/out getting into it, Duncan for, and Bob went with Duncan on the question obviously (that is, as it should be, he wasn't there, plus wasn't that close to Duncan—his invitation I think coming out of that Bard Bl. Mt. thing Duncan read at); next thing was the Olson Memorial by "that minister of Berkeley" (RC), which Bob cancelled—and the whole issue is over the "spiritual" (the Curriculum as you know is of the Soul)—when we were starting out with the C of S Robt Kelly put the project down for dredging up the old question of the soul again and Charles cancelled him, "never darken my door again…" (Fee he cancelled for the Bl Mt Bk mostly)—Creeley & I have always "parted company" on this issue, but it wasn't openly stated because there was no occasion—till now); now, finally, this groundswell of resentment and possessiveness" (RC) has become the occasion, the occasion of the public exposure of different "frames" (Bob's word) of Olson by people who knew him at different "times" in his life. And any "special view" of Olson might be called possessive of him, but I think what has "spooked" Bob (his word) is this what he regards as religious contexting of Olson. When Blake in old age had disciples they called him The Intepreter. That nicely neutral, the man is simply one who interprets things better than anyone else around, someone you can go to etc. Now we all know there are other matters involved here, other transmissions etc. Our problem all along, & maybe Kelly was right in a way, was to leave or propose things in a, for lack of a better term, spiritual vocabulary of enthusiasm in a time of the end of existential humanism. This of course began for me and most others of the C of S long before any association with CO. What is problematic for Bob I think is including his Olson in such dreck (his word), when he has been at pains for some time to "edit out" the kook strain and make Charles available to all (problem is it hasn't worked out that way—by expung-

ing the real agenda of O's work—in the "church forever"—in fact any
theoretical side to it (and you know how such "dogmatic" statements
as that which exists through itself etc can be heard as essentially of an
existential context as in Creeley's things come and go so let them poem,
which is terrific but of another orientation than the Golden Flower say,
among many possible) as extraneous to what the poem itself is saying
(sometimes true, but not as agenda)—anyway the upshot is that O's
work, except for the Ca tomes, is almost unavailable and he's being
taken out of anthologies he was once in). I don't see limiting Charles
to poetry as such or except as such or certainly to Bl Mt Movement in
same or whatever as being useful to keeping him in print and avail-
able. On those criteria he may not even make it. Creeley's and Duncan's
initial response to his verse was the wastebasket. They responded to
his unquestioned authority. From whence does it derive? You say Fate
(not influence), so be it. At least that's a contexting beyond reality as
"the shifting face of need" (Bob's definition back in *The Island*, if you
remember?) It seems to me Bob loves the line from "The Librarian," say,
but would have no interest (public) in what is buried there (& I don't
mean George's love-kins), but the actual "metaphysics" of the ques-
tion (in overall context of the work). And this so-called or thought-of
theoretical side to it does influence this side, e.g., was that even Lufkin's
diner Creeley was in 1966? or had it already become the one that's there
now? As I recall it was already changed (I'll check with Gerrit who will
know). I drove John to Panna's. Mary & I had our honeymoon there.
Panna had not yet arrived. Saw Charles the next 2 day-nights through
(he put Mary to bed in Charles Peter's room). We are breakfast at the
diner the morning we left, Charles doing the Lord's Prayer, which Mary
could of course remember better than he could. And I don't think it
was Lufkin's anymore, no it wasn't. Point is, as in the Moebius Strip,
one side turns into the other easily, and back. And if you don't have
or propose the two, what have you got? Certainly not Olson, who was
a stickler on this point. Biomorphism, the fusion of the 2 sides into
one. He taught, as you know (eg. Last Lectures) always the 2, whether
genetics and morphology or etc., but never what Blake accused WW of,
the atheism of the world of nature. Part of his quarrel with this age is its
putting an a- before everything. Take that out as irrelevant & what have
you got? Charles suckered everybody into the idea he cared about what
the world thought, but by his life, the choices he made, willy nilly even,
you know he didn't really. He was driven surely to & by another out-

come. In the end, although Bob's Olson is more mainstream he doesn't enter the mainstream. That's the paradox. You both may think "my" Olson is off the wall, but I'll bet it will bring him in faster than trying to do it the other way, though it may take awhile (usually at least 100 yrs). Otherwise, this is all just a fight to see who the anthologies and schools will proclaim the successor to Pound & WCW. My Olson is not in that line, but in the Homer-Hesiod-Dante line, but bigger obviously (& not because of God or the gods etc.)—when does 1-A get him home, when the public works dept. changes the road, not likely. Only if you make, like Seymour Knox, money, do you get yr own road home (route 400 it's called). Yet we do demand it, for all. Otherwise we're asking Charles to accept the way it was, Route 128 or whatever, when it ain't, which we all know. enuf. Oh, that Vedic thing, that wasn't scholarship, only common sense, I thought, because we were 120 AD not BC, & Charles had paired the Arabs & Norse in the C of S, "Veda than" is way back, unless you stress the than, or late Buddhist perhaps??? Nothing since sense.

Signing off, JACK.

Jazz Song Sends Species Desire
of Star Woman

The structure of desire (for song) is morphological.

The 3 steps, as *gens*-song, won't satisfy - as Ismael Reed has it, "jes grew" peters out without its "text."

Jazz satisfies the desire for song not the song in itself, the forms of which always fall back into the sexual.

Poetry now must ply the 3 steps morphologically as desire, if it wishes to reach species.

Lacan asked the question, what was Freud's desire? So we must ask, what was Swinburne's?
> what was Whitman's?
> & Pound's?

The evagination of species steps out in 4/4 but without a textual environment to make it right and necessary it is contained in models of "outside" derived from enfranchisements other than species (specific, speculum etc.), which out of fear and to protect itself places song last on the list, whereas humanly it is still first:

> "All art begins in the physical discontent (or torture) of loneliness and partiality . . .
> It is to fill this lack that man first spun shapes out of the void. And with the intensity of this longing gradually came unto him power, power over the essences of the dawn, over the filaments of light and the warp of melody . . .
> Of such perceptions rise the ancient myths of the origin of demi-gods. Even as the ancient myths of metamorphosis rise out of

flashes of cosmic consciousness."

(E.P., San Trovaso Notebook -see page xiv)

Ez had talent for mask, personae, but not as you say "trope.
Monk." It is the sphere of, not power over, the warp of melody.
Blakean rewrite of "Praise of Ysolt": (p xv)

> A woman as fire upon the pine woods
>> crying 'Desire, a desire.'
>>> [the moment of desire]
>> As the flame crieth unto the sap.
>>> My desire was ablaze with her and she went from me . . .

Because if we make desire morphological rather than sexual we can
continue thus :

> And I 'I have no desire,'
> Till my soul sent a song as the sun:

And then step 3 regains—after epistemology and politics
theology - all three thus:

> And I 'I have no desire,'
> Till she [Ysolt] sent a song as the sun

>> rather than

> And I 'I have no song,'
> Till my soul sent a woman as the sun:

These are all promissory notes (non-human) and must be (were) paid
later. So, the final step, is to remove 'I' & restore soul (or species):

> And soul 'soul had no desire,'
> Till Ysolt sent a song as the sun

>>> (which is more accurately a
>>> star)

>> OR

> And species 'species has no desire,'

> Till jazz sends a song as a star

>>> (i.e., a drum is a woman)

Then the original may be restored:

>   And I 'I have no song,'
>   Till my soul sent a woman as the sun

And the lines following are read with the gain (of morphology)

>   Yea as a star calleth to jazz,
>   As the spring upon the bough
>   So is the song that cometh the desire-drawer
>   Song that holdeth the wonder words within species

Here's the actual poetry in case you don't have it:

>   Yea as the sun calleth to the seed,
>   As the spring upon the bough
>   So is she that cometh the song-drawer
>   She that holdeth the wonder words within her eyes . . .

This obviously is a reading exercise, not for writing. The evagination has not been written. Writing will only come when these changes are ingrained (all five of them):

>   desire for song
>   song for woman
>   woman for soul
>   soul for I
>   (species)
>   & star
>   (Sirius)
>   for sun.

Then the headline reads:

JAZZ SONG SENDS SPECIES DESIRE OF STAR WOMAN

>   Osiris---------Horus --- Set -------------- Isis

>   – as Content

>   extended to

>   Form

rather than left as content to be 'carried' by

old genetic metaphor—evaginated [the poetic procedure

given me by phone in Ohio 1979]

poetry can

begin to transact the world, i.e., **hold** *what jes grew*

like Charles' 'violets'

springing up (sans 'blood') –

(that is, most people make ma-conquest but
not pa; poetry conquers pa, but—as Blake
saw—only to leave it with Luvah/Orc

which goes direct to Vala (dream) –

his break-through, the change to *4 Zoas*

& ALBION

Los, the fourth immortal starry one

(Sun, Mercury, Venus, *Ear*th

Why Ez's "Revolt: Against the Crepuscular Spirit in Modern Poetry"
(see page xi)—

"I would shake off the lethargy of this our time, and give
For shadows—shapes of power   [Los is the
For dreams—men.   figure of time]

OKAY, BUT. . .

"But my soul sent a woman, a woman of the wonderfolk"
(p xv)

translates

ORC SENT VALA THE EMANATION OF LUVAH

(IN Jung terms, the defeat of the Shadow recoils as defeat by
the *anima*, so instead of wise men you get:

revolutionaries bound
to the dream of history

Beginning the modern with *Marriage of Heaven and Hell* ("energy is eternal delight" & is from the body etc.) instead of following where that energy went post the 4-Zs (*Milton* & *Jerusalem*) is truly going off half-cocked.

It went to FORM:

JERUSALEM SENDS ALBION LOS FROM ENITHARMON

    (song)   (species) (poet) (star)

Leaving out desire-woman-soul until we are strong enough to bring them in. At the moment when we look at the urn we are still liable to see two people kissing instead, so no sense trying to carry these contents until mental stability achieved (which to accomplish we need new mind).

Until poetry makes a text (of words) equal to jazz (song)

    what is said of what is said (O.)

    – the Centauric instruction
    which reduces to

    Dawn and Cloud
    (muspil)   (nifl)

    [the instruments of creation]

we won't be p-mod. And this requires belief in mythology, as Lawrence knew.

Blake Was a Genius at It

Blake was genius at it

imagine saying, straight out

as you live

"From every one of the four
        regions of human majesty"

{why Charles said he's post-mod
        & belongs to 21st Century}

        he had all four going
he saw them
he heard them
he knew who
        they were
                (could name

_____

could address time
(& those of it) which would
        be that "going reality"
children of the happier
age, when sweet love
        not thought a crime

which you say. As of Eden,

'I used to think
    it was to simply
        name
        /

well, what:?

[Jack Clarke to Al Glover
postmarked 2/24/1977]

ON WRITING
(CORRESPONDENCE)

Feb 23 1987

Dear Kedrick –

Your letter & poem (which I liked) just in. Let me requote the Coleridge proposition (from *The Friend*) I started with: "progressive transition without breach of continuity," and then quote Henry Corbin (from "The Concept of Comparative Philosophy," (Golgonooza Press, 1981), as of what Sloan was calling in that Review "accepted notions of the self," or what has passed for "continuity" since the 17th century, marked by the "hiatus" between (Arab) alchemy and modern chemistry, Corbin:

What appeared to us after the event as a continuity was in fact only a succession of discontinuous leaps, of new points of departure each time unforeseeable . . .. I have the feeling that the geometrical configuration of qualitative forms in Nicholas Oresme is not, in the proper sense of the word, any more a preliminary chapter to analytical geometry, than alchemy is the prehistory of modern chemistry. In order to have this last, as we have said, Descartes was necessary. But there was no necessity that there should be a Descartes after a Nicholas Oresme. Descartes' appearance was a new event, a discontinuity.

My point is, breaching the "succession of discontinuous leaps"—so important to the art & science of this century, which Olson called "cinematic"—is not the same as breaching actual continuity, which, as the Xanadu-Poet says, poetry doesn't do. Poetry only participates in discontinuity (despite Eliot's tying the 17th century "dissociation" [a term of chemistry] of sensibility" to its tail) to that extent that it, too, finds itself in the 'space' opened up by this usurpation of "the moment of transition" (Corbin). The ribbon of tradition the individual talent is thereby free/bound to cut into is already a breach of continuity, a succession (success) of new points of departure.

Blake, in the *Four Zoas* had already by the end of the 18th century rewritten the 'historical' record to include this event of Corbin's, and had informed poetry of its proper response to it. That is, when Urthona at his forge hears the sounds of war between Urizen & Luvah (Western Phallologocentrism?), he drops his hammer, and until picked up by the blacksmith Los the activities of actual time are suspended. This "event" repeats itself, and has, every time form becomes so removed from its 'content' that it can be appropriated by other contents. Writing itself would be 'first' instance, as it emerged out of those Neanderthal arts you mention, dance, sculpture, painting, etc. (for which see Alexander Marshack's work on the "time-factoring" of remains of all such activity). That is, inscription didn't come about—a simple fact we forget because of our phonological bias—to record either speech or the things & events of the world. Only when emptied of its own 'meaning' could it be put to these other uses. I take this thought direct from Husserl's "The Origin of Geometry," which I may as well also quote to you, so you will be clear about its application to poetry-as-writing, that is, long before the so-called oral tradition, when the discoveries were made, say, that the moon records a process, as Marshack believes, which falls to the poet to 'equal' (Los builds it "plank by plank") but, as we know, not without also June & spoon etc., for it is the combinatory access of these different "writings" and their homologies that empowers poetry still, in spite of the acoustic metaphor people like to think is its only difference from the prosaic languages they have acquired, Husserl:

> Without the actually developed capacity for reactivating the original activities contained within its fundamental concepts, i.e., without the 'what' and the 'how' of its prescientific materials [writing], geometry would be a tradition empty of meaning; and if we ourselves did not have this capacity, we could never even know whether geometry had or ever did have a genuine meaning, one that could really be 'cashed in.'

> Unfortunately, however, this is our situation, and that of the whole modern age. . . .

> The capacity for reactivating the primal beginnings, i.e., the sources of meaning for everything that comes later, has not been handed down with it. . . .

> Thus mathematics, emptied of meaning, could generally propagate itself, constantly being added to logically, as could the methodics of technical application on the other side. The extraordinarily far-reaching practical usefulness became of itself

a major motive for the advancement and appreciation of those sciences.

That's enough, you get my point, that not only the "writing" that became geometry (the entry into whose meaning is lost, though not its use-value), but writing itself, handed down to those who could not 'read' it, thus empty of its own warnings, was used to 'say', and thereby fix the saying of, almost everything else, language, nature, history, you name it. I am using writing at this very moment in that manner, & I agree with your own impatience (if not with your versa vica pun), when you had to simply STOP . . . and "offer" "writing", which had only to be a poem, which had only to be, what I think I'm trying to say here, is numbers, that what the original meaning of writing and what we mean by poetry share or have in common is number, and so what Husserl above is saying about mathematics is not as far removed from poetry as it might seem. To use your word, poetry has to do with "recounting," with counting and re-counting, even as those first "writings", which were not spoken nor yet tied to "associatively derived falsifications" (Husserl), but were like 'stampings' (oven of dancing feet) that by some miracle of morphogenesis 'engraved' in whatever substance, earth itself, that same 'river' Heraclitus would say you don't step twice into. That through writing had been discovered "a passing from one world to another" (Corbin) at the point of hiatus, that point of numerical transition, just there, where otherwise the breach occurs, where continuity (with the dead) is lost, because writing had suddenly been mads to serve other ends than its own. Every new departure is an attempt to step into that same river (of time); only those "strange steps" "little steps" can match those 'notches' in the brain through which Alph ran—why Robert Graves says it's death to love a poet, to be a poet, & to cross a poet.

Again, best, John Clarke

May 7, 1987

Dear Tina,

Keep separate

"the challenge i
    can recognize   /   WRITING
    for poetry"

save, for now   just write, as *always*
doing intros etc.   w/out regard for
                    "an answer"

In other words, construct
a/the "sound barrier" between –
& low & behold, as Ornette Coleman says, sound story!
That is, "resolve to posit" that separation, so none
of
    THIS SIDE   leaks through to   THE OTHER SIDE

Paradox: By doing this, strenuously, the two will,
    one day, come together and/or be the *same*. But
    for now any interference from one to the other
    only generates unfounded doubts & fears

So, turn doubt / fear into the barrier itself, as though
    to say, if I cross that line I'm dead, or my life as
    writer anyway. The fact that *you* construct it, though
    not arbitrary, that is, no less inflexible than,
    makes it less scary, than UNIVERSE, say.

Or, another way to say it (say it—WCW) is that
    poetry is *not* recognition —

no in fact, cogito, but
as you have it: I write, therefore I is. Not
for public consumption (Emily D)—or to say, if going
to heaven might as well be a/the real one!

It wasn't the tip of the iceberg (what critics wrangle about, i.e., poems) that sank the Titanic anyway. Or, to return to the *ground* for the "unknown" story, notice how the ground-hog only occasionally and quite warily poketh he head out of him hole where he do liveth.

Simply resolve to be ½ smart—which dissolves the smart/dumb "duality" which always creates crisis of confidence *in anyone*. Don't judge, draw line. And abide.

Writing gets you to where you're going, *by indirection*. What you will think end come to say about L=A=N=G requires no positing of PCS, you who are her protectress.

I liked the way you applied the Blake four-fold to the discussion there. Good framing device, for starters.

Love, & belief, JACK

Aug. 28 1986

Dear Tina –

Novalis asks a great question, namely:

"It would be a nice question to determine whether the lyric poem is
actually poetry."

Here is his answer:

"The highest, truest prose is the lyric
poem."

Check it out.

Poetry, on the other
hand, he says,

"should result in a system of tropes, a tropology, which would encom-
pass the rules of the . . .
construction of the . . .
world."

Dig that!   Trope/Rule/World

So we are back to Olson's old question: how many? and

how *each* made known?

Some definitions:

Tropology (for Olson) is the turning in response to the
'queerness' of yrself.

(the Jack Nicholson problem: "It's very hard for me
to find a place to put my individual foot down where I
don't know how one of the great masters does it already")

Otherwise, it's all Sunflower . . . weary of time.

Clue: stay with myth, and away from folktale —

Persephone is eternally unique

> (system of tropes here goes back to at least Sumerian "Descent of Inanna" in preserved text, further w/out writing)

> OK, as to the rules of the construction of the world— Novalis again:

"You realize that what is projected here is an infinite measure. There are two variable factors that stand in augmenting interrelation to one another and whose product advances hyperbolically. But to make this image clearer, we must bear in mind that we are dealing not with movement and expansion in a quantitative fashion but with an ennobling variation (differentiation and separation) of qualities we call nature."

A doubt creeps in: Will my trope-inventory somehow produce an entry into this qualitative variation of cosmos (what since Alfred North Whitehead we have come to call "Process and Reality")?

Another due: (this time from Friedrich Schlegel)

"It is equally deadly for a mind to have a system or to have none. There it will have to decide to combine both."

For, as he says in his 19th C. vocabulary,

> "In every good poem, everything must be both deliberate and instinctive. That is how the poem becomes ideal."

> Upshot: You don't have a sting without the bee

> > (no matter you may have scorpio in yr chart).

> > For trope-bee, see Kerenyi's Dionysos—or wait for From *Feathers to Iron* to arrive (October?).

> > Schlegel also says:

"Publication is to thinking as confinement is to the first kiss."

(Note: the first kiss is between Lancelot and Guinevere, not Guinevere and Arthur—but, again, as Schlegel says: "Women have to remain prudish as long as men are sentimental." He prefers Sappho, and Antigone, to Penelope.)

Well, is this enough German Romanticism for one day? Especially, in the middle of raspberry season, no less.

> *My prince waits in a field of flowers blowing.*—GREAT LINE

> (See Cocteau's "Beauty and the Beast")

One last Schlegelism:

> "In the invention of details, your own imagination is rich enough: to stimulate it, to excite it to activity, and to provide it with nourishment there is nothing better than the creations of other artists."

So, if imagination =s the (your) 'system of tropes', then
the activity here is the 'construction of the world'.

For, as Novalis says, "When the laggard is set into motion, he is all the more daring and irrepressible."

> This, then, would mean "negative capability" +
> the Tinatrope =s poetry.

All love, J.

Jan 26 1987

Dear Duncan,

Since marriage is further than death (my paraphrase of DHL in *Lots of Doom.* 1971), the whole morta-cluster would have to be broken into "to kill."

qwel [2]—to pierce

(interesting that *qwel* [3] brings up glans—acorn*
(as I have in *From Feathers to Iron* from
the Friedrich *Aphrodite*

& *qwel* [4]   to fly; a wing
(as in "winged" thought & to kiss the joy
as it flies   [glans?

& *qwel* [5]   to swallow   (how swallow it?

& then back to *qwel* [1]   to throw, reach

boule (Cf. O's "fly up, fly out . . ." of
the drum poem for me in MF5

determination, will "throwing forward of
the mind"
(cf. Blake's intellectual arrows, darts,
etc. (atl-atl)

(not that you're supposed to do this
with the dictionary, but does promote
thought as cluster 'of five'
(cf. "you five" of the
Samothrace mystery—
which wld be like "your" picture from Zimmer, but taking the
arms of the Ladie of 1st Kiss as those of Hainuwele, i.e., one

side for fivers the other for niners, so to have dif. between the
"way" of the dis., and the Way of This . . .
(1971-1987)

The "number" of *actual* time (as DHL has it in that Christmas letter
Glover pub., I can't find, also mentioned in *Lots of Doom*) is SEVEN.
Look at my piece for Pauline Wah in Dan's *Western Gate*:

7 - "to pierce through with or fix
on something" (as of 2-18-70)

So if you can pierce through there |
with something like the kiss of mistletoe* that killed
your Baldr the Beautiful, on what do you then fix?
I would cut here direct to *Call Me Ishmael* on first
murder—the actual dark deed, not Freud's speculum, not Father &
Sons, but "what's back there," as in the sense of 7th Nommo 'dying' for
the 8th (As with Hainuwele, the burial, in matter, & cf. last letter as
to what *was* slain in the sun, and from the foundation, the fundament
itself . . .

Ishmael for 'tone'; for event back to the (your) LION GATE
—thus to assure an indirect approach, so old death does not strike fear
where marriage protects flank in the act of piercing through itself, like a
Valentine.

J.

August 25 1985

Harvey,

I was thinking for the book, or *a* book, yes probably the 'travel'–book to come out of yr sense of south axis (on the 'American' side), anyway,

to study (for organization of material etc.) the 'plan' Charles drew up for the Guggenheim application,

so you might start with the Jaguar, jade-stone of Chichen Itza, or deeper in jungle—did you ever get that book of Gertrude Reichel-Dolmatoff I had, *The Shaman & the Jaguar?*—for the Amazonian stuff,

and make right from the head that connection to "Cats," cool or otherwise (Kulkulkan? hmm), you intuited, as a direct line to the present

lead in, because that's what you/we want now obviously, not the past, archaeo or anthro etc.,

unless your own as relevant almost anecdote etc., what it was like to drive your own Jaguar, sleek black into the dawn—

almost like a fourfold cluster: jungle experience (like that Wizard book that I guess was another 'hoax', but no matter);

the stone works (Yucatan etc., on site);

you, as such (having unknowing lived, i.e., by simple fact of choices, in this 'world' before you knew);

& the "playing" and players,

CATS,

Pres et.al., that is yr subject,

so that hovering around the *chac mool,* or whatever the center of this cluster at the moment, there are these other strains at the edges, especially *you* —

not only as where the poems wld naturally come in, but stories not yet written,

      so all instances of "Jaguar" that comprise this first unit would be there as entrance (en-tranced into that *place*—
which Charles could never write, not only because he followed Ez into 'history', but because he had *town* as place.

      You have no such restriction on you, so I'd make use of, that is, practically, what he outlined to do but could never do, as the *onlie* (lonely) CAT of Gloucester (writing about DOGS instead).

      When you go to Merida, take along a notebook whose pages can be divided (not as we had it previously divided into two) but divided) into *four* columns--Burroughs I guess had his divided into three (I'll run his down on the next page)--but, still, *all* Jaguar. Then the next cluster to follow according to plan, whatever it is, which is where the study of organization comes into direct application, specific to your dream etc.

Burroughs says: "One column will contain simply an account of my trip, what happened . . . what was said . . . The next column presents my memories: that is what I was thinking at the time, the memories that were activated by my encounters. And the third column, which I call my reading column, gives quotations from any book that I take with me

      "I do a lot of exercises in what I call time travel . . . to see how completely I can project myself back in time." *Paris Review* Interview, Writers at Work, 3rd Series.

Since you're dealing with space, not time (per se), you'll be going in the opposite direction, and projecting yourself forward in time rather than backward. You already have the "back in time," what you want is the present—the Jaguar World in the present. Also, this will mean the opposite of memories activated by encounters. Instead, the memories will be actively brought *to* the encounters, for it is "there" that has forgotten, and been forgotten, not "here," like anthro in reverse, almost—but with *enthymesis* instead of how Ez reversed it by telling people what to do etc. There may not be a convenient (good) precedent for it, Apple of T. isn't one either, D. Cherry better for sure, but only on one of the tracks (professionally).

Writing this just reminded me of the Pound/Frobenius connection, and how Ez thought they were cats! (H.D. goes into this a bit, too, in her book on Ez)—but obviously they weren't Cats (I don't know what that was about, Eliot, too, and his cats?—must be simply mimetic or thorough-going simple location vs.

Place, i.e..

The Place Where the Jaguar Priests Go,

in the old formula, now the geography (in Irby's sense) of the sound

traced to

the source of the river=

the burning desire any cool (cool or fool) cat has inside of him—

that you bring to these former times and places to restore the continu-ity—that there is "no break," as Charles said in the "Atlantis" poem (Melkarth etc.)—that the Jaguar world is here if our desire and belief is strong enough to sustain the year (as Herakles is fabled to have done), which reminds me of another Olson poem—you published—the *Ocean.*

Anyway, the steps between Jaguars and cats is the work (labors?), and it will always go on, year after year, but the leap into form is always now, immediate and present. We are no longer preparatory to convic-tion. If we don't have that thing to suck (you know the one, nothing, but something like ripples) by *now*, then we are either still sucked off or sucked in by what we want.

Blake translation: Vala will always be jealous of Jerusalem as long as Albion hides her in Tharmas. That is, the four Rivers, Senses, of Paradise.

Done, J

Jesus H. Clarity:

Ah men. Ioway was the last of it for me, *personally*, when both of them, Creel and Anselm invaded my Rebel room. The ghost of O coming in like Omlet's father saying with sneer voice etc. like Lew doesn't rime with lush at Berkeley. Then R.D. later chiming, we never knew until he was dead, as of Spicer. These ha-ha voices, as inner whisper, coupled with the absolute blindness (in your sense of the word) of say Dorn, curiously, as of heroes, opened up the archaic gap between fire & water

the niner where Titans are, thus the dry tree, and windy place Odin was hung for poetic runes

so giving ground *cosmologique* replacing (*not* deposing, as you have the Jung statement as of *Orphee*) the former psychologische of person

P E R S O N A L I T Y — I E S

which kept us (royally) screwed by that very mumbo-jumbo of "inner" supposition and thus away from what Blake noticed was WAR (Cf. your Burroughs piece) —

dig what I'm saying, "cult of personality" lets it *all* off the hook, both ways, i.e., *now* that you have the clarity (was that Don Juan's second enemy? anyway the next step, then, is the power(s)—our struggle is not with flesh etc. of the opening of *The Four Zoas*—which means the awful (wretch) job of placing this steady recognition into its

M Y T H O L O G I C A L C O S M O L O G I C A L

otherwise here known as the "work" (to do), which as every major writer since Goethe knows is PUBLIC (Blake calling it the delivery of Individuals from States—

States of Sleep, 3x9=27, not angels, or even titans, but fully human (however banal the lady thought evil of the 20th snuff) beings under-the-influence of HATE, as in Ragnarok, brother will eat brother etc.

Why terms, "hype," "ego," "inflation," "personality" (with cult as only metaphor) are too weak to hold the other term (or pole) of your contrary. If the "work" is cosmos, then its negative side, as "habit" or "addiction," must (equally) be better specified within the WORK IT-SELF. Otherwise the work is not applied where it most counts, and the criminal again gets off by pleas of insanity (*temporary*, e.g. I was drunk).

Putting "inner supposition" in its best light, I suppose, and god knows it is in a dark place, like Blake's "forests of night," it would be analogous to the X, as Olson has it:

> to tear love loose

Or, as in Blake, Albion will not leap into the furnace of affliction without that overshadowing of the Covering Cherub which constitutes the danger to friends.

Or, you have it as "loathly" (Charles' Indian lady as the fire-water bath figure under human analogy) which prompts the tongue out of "vegetation" (in this case the bio-morphism called psychology) into the language of love, love triumphant! (Which is what I meant in those talks about applying the proposition.)

In other words, you have (already) a complete system one of whose "units" can accommodate and specify this going on, this "unfinished" reality, so don't let the shrinks slip in (to your mind) to steal it away.

This in fact may be where Charles started with Merry. The State of Drunkenness in which you find the one you're with, so much so you speak ('unawares' as STC did once) not to save self but the spell -bound tongue, which thereby releases friend as well, what Novalis calls a double transformation.

> 1) juice as Nile slime made cosmological
> 2) seed cast as poetic language
> 3) increase of society through human friendship

the Shakespearean methodology I learned from you, fair, kind, true, or as O put it, there is no further movement into the (sick) rose of the world w/out the Aesir-Vanir, ie,

the inclusion of nifl (humanly what to whom, as whomever one is (stuck) with or on), as full (of drink) twin to muspil overshadowed (covered, fused etc.) until earthling in question can act to extricate mutuality further than old pre-war assumption permits. This is the end of the world, beyond duality (Duessa), where lions roam.

Thus the barrow so much depends upon. *You* are responsible, *your* act of mind (dissertation itself) created the present reality you confront, EROS restored to cosmology, wrested from psychology (liquor is quicker); simply (ha!) return your children to their text. I wouldn't let him get away etc. Recalim, that's *reclaim* the furnaces (hells), Los sole lord of, no creation (impossible) that isn't highest intensity, reap the harvest or tears of woe you'll surely wipe, your turn or you wouldn't feel it so, the weird responsibility come true! Post-asshole Urizen you are Fathar. Human grapes sing not in the Wine-press. They hate us for abandoning them, you know.

As poets we live in the Blake Age. All depends upon that *belief.* All of O's exploration *within* that creation, though he went 'back' & 'forth' to re-fish, as say "Sumer" & "Alfred North Whitehead", and was perhaps too Catholic ever to believe anything but "the Greatest Story," even the Jung quaternity really father, son, virgin, & spirit for him, rather than Zoa-fourfold or terms of "vision" as in Blake.

Didn't matter, he nonetheless brought most of that "eternity" into the world as anyone since. Our job, as children of both, was as you say the work of that belief. You going (as Blake did) to original instance in Shakes., and Glove to Milton (again as Blake), me working the B-O axis, and all of us with Lawrence, so that the comprehension of this human transfer through the word became more explicit in the 70's after Charles . . .

I won't be able to do that job until George's Biography of O is done. In the meantime those who have no belief must be tended to, or it's going to get ugly. That is, Creeley, for example is against the "I just work here" philosophy, but he really doesn't know why that is, or even who Mr. Blue is? or his famous "content" etc. He assumes the world, which has been all our habit. That world is fading fast, which is making people take to new habits. But, as I say, the reason it is fading is the signal Blake sent up the smoke hole with *Milton*, the beginning of the Human Universe.

All of us have been hung-up in the old niner where Blake himself was in *The Four Zoas* (actually *Vala*, as the title change registered the change I'm going on here, which occurred at Felpham), Olson

included because I think he couldn't get through *Billy Budd* of his man
(as Blake said embraces must be comingling from head to toe, for which
Charles leaves the human and goes to the turgor of tips and ends, again
left in the world, not the H.U.). All of which you were at pains to point
out in L.T., i.e., your own 'megalithic' apologia, but in none of these
cases has it stopped the work.

        In your case, you proposed the full
traversal, right up to and including the final fiver with Dionysos (and
thus the drama of it you've been doing since), which acts of mind and
language brought into being more of the "plan"; therefore, you will also
take the heat or backlash of those for whom the rug (ala the bear) has
been pulled, Blake's "starry floor," those "Jobs" who refuse to accept the
plan, who consider brotherhood a social term of bondage, like Hell's
Angels or other unconscious perversions of responsibility which cast
the eternal seed upon stones rather than take the trouble to locate the
specific ground of same (Job's Elihu of plate 12). It is of course Milton
they all really hate, not you, because he wrote the epic. It's as Charles
said (in last secret notes) at such a low even everybody is going to have
to CHANGE. Blake was simply the one to have to change first.

    Another way to express the change (had come) is North-South
replacing East-West (Wheel of Religion, and solar analogy generally,
kings etc.), which I try to cover in those lectures, & why Poe, the Pym
stuff for sure, by Mr. Drink, Mr. Eversion hisself.

So it's not the al'cohol per se or as such, but the "inner supposition," as
existentialism which Chas sd. was only a complaint that the pigs had
won.

    And not to get into Circean barley matter, pigs taste, they say, very
like human. Pigs close to human. Why I guess, as of the inhumanity of
the Angel, Melville said: all are Ahab. Or remember Piggy in *Lord of the
Flies*?

        This then opens into the 3 Classes:

            The Elect—who won't believe (even the plan)

            The Reprobate—tygers

            The Redeemed—pigs

After this "Puritan" mixed gov't came restoration of kings, which was
impossible, they having already left the world stage in Shakespeare.
Why Blake so honored Tom Paine for noticing the king was in his

head, or his house on his head. But even after revolutions, still that CHANGE never got registered as cosmological almost till Olson said *substance*. This was certainly part of Blake's anti-Newtonianism, that it was the axis shift that ended alchemy that he cashed in on and deflected from human use. Both Boehme and Paracelsus seem to have known something of this shift, and got in trouble. One could almost Brooksie this, and show how the E-W routes, no longer policed, by like Enki, were up for grabs (now we call it the credibility gap), while the N-S in our hands became the yuk-yuk of ha ha hee,

which is what

SANDERS understands

& why Olson, & all of us, so value him, throb

like upper and lower Egypt, talk about that Shakespearean slime!

Read

American Hieroglyphics for how the whole of Matty's Ren. learned to write

(I use the Crete version in the lectures because I figure everyone knows something of the Egyptian by now, plus I wanted to pull writing away from the star-river thing into the fully human, ala Heraclitus' you can't wash mud out with mud, or what H. don't know is night & day are same etc., however that might translate out?)

Sanders, I just remembered, is in Rochester tonight!

So (I'm getting tired), but did want to make 5. Because it seems it is the niner (in us, not them, whoever they were) that is angry at the fiver. The Elect of the Retard, in other words, don't like to be replaced by Humanity Awake. Humanity Asleep they like, because then they have it both ways, like really replaced but not deposed! The threat they feel today is from the choice for our Champion, not the Cosmos itself, or *God*

which,

as Blake says, only Acts and Is

in existing beings or Men

that's OK too (scarf), but write that act into the world as work, and you depose the inner king who has not advanced to commonwealth, or what O called another kind of Nation

a Republic in gloom

which is OK (again), because his history not placed, and so not grounded UNTIL post-1970 we begin to notice, again Heraclitus, their life is our death (sleep), talk about UNACKNOWLEDGED legislators.

Addiction is to what you called the "dead angel." He is the K. Billy killed him. Starry Veritas evaginates the good man, like your Baldr, one part to Eternity, the other to be distributed here (*If* Albion awakes in US), completing B's mitosis.

As you know Thokk is Loki in disguise, Blake has it Religion hid in War, or Rahab, Whore of Babylon Pierre saw in the window, who always gets blamed,

> like the Prunikos (any of them),

> Our Lady of the Wild Beasts,

But it is really the False Tongue of anyone who won't complete the hermeneutic circle, what Hawthorne called the magnetic chain, that connecting the 19th to the 17th, no Chill, hush Hester, Dim out, go Pearl!

And to clear up that title, it means the Deeming of the Pearl, that is the doom, the wise-doom upon us, just the reverse of Lawrence's reading of the text. Pearl's difference is she has no Religion in her, which is most likely why Melville thought Hawthorne deeper than Dante, because even Noah had to let Oc ride in on his ark, whereas Pearl, as a human potentiality, has no internal dialogue, and thus no entropy. Lawrence was trodden out by the War, but not Religion. He says, the days of thy interference are over almost as a sneer rather than a quiet truth, with some fear, because if He put off the evil on the cross (as cosmological narrative), what are we still doing with the impossible absurdity in our mouths?

> Overhearing Cass watching Sat. Night Live., voice comes in to Dan A. at typewriter w-out paper,

YOU CAN'T WRITE THE NEWS WHEN YOU'RE ASLEEP

Thinking of P's make it, new   &   O's   taking up his poetry as history that stays news & then some good news can come from C   & Creel's constant person rating as 'good news' it seems a very nice sentence to end with

> N orth

> E ast

W est

S outh

(Cf. plate 98 of *J.*)

For THEN (as in your maybe we can have lunch now),

a person can drink. To reverse the Jung, the E-W is deposed but not replaced, as Zoas of indestructible human life,

so when Ur-thona & Ur-izen meet

Luvah & Tharmas they refuse to recognize any but their eternal form, and none of their exploited "supposition" of the last 200 years, which is a manageable unit of:

cult (anthro

personality (psycho

The mice (non-writers in the sense of not knowing their

predecessors, nor in many cases even their subject)

who played while the cat was away, thus flooded the

world, as Duncan says, equivocally, Fraser and Freud.

This is the struggle now, the clarity of what you have already written against what they have written, which is powerful helpless except the habit of mind to let them have it.

But Ed is saying, even now, "never again." History belongs to poets and nobody else, even if poets don't know it, or want the responsibility, because they like the lazy boho power they all feed on: a body of doubt.

Well, I'd better end this ramble, she's got Star Trek, the final frontier going in there. See what it's about. Didn't catch Ronnie today. He wants to drink from dry glasses alright.

You sound so good and clear, sorry to drop all this on you, not heavily, but just anything that might disturb you from whatever, though I think it's time to notice and thereby believe you have changed not only yourself but the world & time.

Running off the edge of which, Jack.

AFTERWORD

KNOWING JACK

Daniel Zimmerman

In *Anonym* 4 (1969), Jack Clarke published excerpts from Blake's *Milton* and *Jerusalem* as

BLAKE/EPISTEMOLOGY: STANCE I

Distance

Milton 15: 21-35

Constance

Milton 40: 32-37; 41: 1-2; 25-26; 32-36

Instance

Jerusalem 55: 36-46

Substance

Jerusalem 12: 46-50; 57-58; 14: 25-28

(All lines from Keynes)[1]

I read this arrangement as follows:

Distance: Heaven: the past Vortex, where we didn't die / Earth: the future Vortex, where we do. In our *intermediate* distance, we confuse causes and effects; the Vortices resolve them if we comprehend the nature of their

Substance: Golgonooza: the golden builders create the spiritual Jerusalem by opening three gates to each other (in Calabi-Yau-like spaces?) in "Childhood, Manhood & Age." This mitigates somewhat the cause/effect confusion, but the Babel-like mangling of tongues of the Western Gate's closure persists, a Serresian *parasite* (Blake's Devourer), enemy of

Constance: Contraries: they contend to annihilate the spectral Negation, the (confused) reasoning power (first instance: *if* you eat from the Tree, *then* you will become like God). This error inaugurates the Sexual, *as opposed to* Friendship, whose Human Lineaments it figleafs. Until "severe contentions" annihilate that *intermediate* Spectre, we cannot restore true

Instance: "This will come to pass by an improvement of sensual enjoyment. But first the notion that man has a body distinct from his soul is to be expunged," Blake says. Fallen (sexualized) reason reduces the world to dust, impervious to sensual enjoyment. For

> If Perceptive organs vary, Objects of
> Perception seem to vary;
> If the Perceptive Organs close, their Objects
> seem to close also. (*J* 34: 55-56)

Contracting and expanding, our Human Organs shake the dust from the plow and reveal the "weeping clods"—dust reanimated by our labors in the "Moment in each Day that Satan cannot find" (*M* 35: 42).

Years later, this Stance became instrumental for me in *Post-Avant*:

THE MUNDANE SHELL

you never know the entire story
passing the worn cup

the sliver passed from mother to child
emerges only in the child's old age

it goes out like a light in the hands ahead of us

past the sky
down under the earth
clouds
animals of night
ask to be made stars
& fall in with similar companions

hoping nevertheless to avoid bloodshed
until we forget all but the roots' insistence

over the Great Divide & out the Vortex

II: CHOPS

In *From Feathers to Iron: A Concourse of World Poetics*, Jack proposed keeping "four or five interacting analogues" active; for example, in his Prologue to that book, John Thorpe mentions

HECATONCHEIRES

   XVARNAH

     LTALALTUMA

  GOLEM

HOUNGAN

      (xvii).

To add a fifth term to the work proposed in Stance 1, consider John Layard on the Devouring Ghost, Le-hev-hev, & the Path:

I now wish to call your attention to the remarkable test to which the Female Devouring Ghost subjects the ghost of the dead man at the entrance to the Cave. She has drawn with her finger, in the sand, a geometric figure, and she sits beside it, waiting for the dead man to come. He sees her from a distance. He is confused at the sight of her, and loses his way. When he regains his path and approaches the Devouring Ghost, she rubs out half the design. The dead man must know how to complete it. If he succeeds,

> <Fig. i. "The Path" or "The Way." This is the design drawn in the sand by the Female Devouring Ghost. The figure consists of a single continuous line drawn around a framework of straight lines. As soon as the dead man approaches, the Devouring Ghost rubs out half the design, which the dead man must complete before he can pass through the middle of the sand-tracing in the direction indicated by the arrow. (South West Bay, Malekula.)>

he passes through the lines of the geometric design into the Cave. If he does not succeed, he is devoured by the terrible ghost.

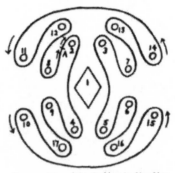

Dance pattern of the Goddess Le-Hev-Hev

Figure i is an illustration of the design she draws, which the natives of all these islands also draw sometimes in the sand; it is called "The Path," which might be better translated "The Way." First a framework of straight lines is drawn. Around and within this framework a continuous line is traced; the finger must under no circumstances be taken off until the design is complete. (137)

In "The Strengthening Method of World Completion," Jack quotes Wittgenstein on this matter: "I understand a proposition by *applying it*" (154), and notes that " . . . in The Faerie Queen . . . a central figure, Red Cross, having reached the end of his rope, is displaced by Arthur. Blake completes the other half of the picture in *Jerusalem* when Albion (Arthur) awakens to Jesus, who is 'identified' with Los" (155). Jack long ago gave me Walter Jackson Bate's *The Burden of the Past and the English Poet*, which anticipates "the progress of poetry' as a matter of what Harold Bloom calls *misprision*—deliberate (?) misreading of strong predecessors. The Strengthening Method offers, as Blake did in *Milton*, completion rather than negation as a way further. When the dead Malekulan initially experiences (rational) confusion at the sight of Le-hev-hev, negation will doom him; completion alone—of his *own* figure—can save him. Unlike negation (which implies a thoroughly symmetrical opposite), completion (by contrariety) may entail an asymmetrical response. In "The True Vine," Jack wrote that

> Jesus' radicalism was in his disconcern with high or low levels of past performance as a yo-yo, his sword cut that hanging judge situation, his point was to bring nothing more than you to his transaction, to invest your pieces with enough energy that you could feel the present level (baptism), that only this wine of love could relieve you of your doom. (*FFtI* 10)

The poet-as-Malekulan does not have to complete the figure by remembering the obliterated half (knowing does not necessarily mean remembering), but by imagining its completion strongly enough to convince the Devouring Ghost that, like Dante in Hell, he has not really died and, therefore, does not qualify as lunch.

I see the Malekulan fifth term as a factor of Blake's Western Gate, the (closed) gate of the tongue but also the gate of touch, a persistent finger linking the other four Stance 1 dimensions. Jack contributed the following poem to my magazine, *The Western Gate*:

JC: **The Opening of the Western Gate Upanishad**

for *Daniel John Zimmerman*

THARMAS—on what is he based?
On water.
And on what is water based?

On semen.
And on what is semen based?
On the heart.
"Cf. 'The Heart as a Subtile Organ' Henry Corbin *Ibn 'Arabi*, p. 221
His heart's his mouth
What his breast forges, that his
Tongue must vent.

Spring 1970

DZ: **guide book**

places of interest clearly marked, Scenic Overlook,
Slough of Despond, itinerary inked in fluorescent green,
equally appropriate, that meteoric fireball I saw with Jack
en route to Goddard to read for Grossinger's crowd
of earwaxed rowers who must've thought us booty
at first, then windbags--Glover, Jack, me, & Harvey Brown
each taking solos, ready though unbidden to jam in Q & A.
we read into noise silent as snow, as dark matter holds
the universe together, spoke into canyons unfathomable
trusting eventual echoes to strengthen homeopathically
titrated by shakeups of expectation in the Voids
between the Stars obsessively scrutinized till constellations
loom, refocused by the Magic Eye on loan from the poets,
yours to keep till you reach the shore, & then return.

III: INSPECTING THE LYRE

Still, as Ralph Maud has said, "[n]othing grates more than a disciple's
sympathetic rephrasing of one's ideas" (Maud). I tried to keep that yet
unpublished caveat in mind when Cass Clarke generously invited me to
respond to some of Jack's yet-unpublished sonnets from *In the Analogy*,
remembering, too, that Jack had written to me while directing my
dissertation, "[d]on't forget that as you wield the four-fold you are that
penultimate 'complex occasion' not yet discriminated (till post-1950)
ETC." (qtd. in *blue horitals*). In the following call and response from
that collaboration, I sought fidelity to that twin determination:

JC: **<u>Cleros-Sphota</u>***

Tiresias was blinded by the wrong question,
Oedipus, too, too easily right, boringly sage
in a place that poo-poo'd Cassandra's attempt

to jog their thinking, what got us all going
professionally in what wasn't one, a mystery
that alone might strengthen what is taken
for granted or lost to the above glibnesses,
allowing the echo of other fine solutions
to make light of the distances Evil traverses
to get to us, or so one supposes who knows
the difference between heartbreak & lost love,
Lawrence comes to mind as one who's undergone
the harrowing, wouldn't lose him to Pound—
taking off together into the wild blue yonder.

Sept 18 1991

* A lot of Zeus *noos.*

"If the subject is Cassandra it is interesting to note that she
differs, for instance, from the tragic heroine of Aeschylus or
Euripides in not delivering her prophecies in ecstatic verse,
but standing in a dignified pose and drawing a lot."

H. W. Parke, "Dodona," *The Oracles of Zeus*

"The original monuments of perception
are the play of light
through the wall's membrane."

Edward Dorn, *Recollections of Gran Apacheria*

"The image or persona, what is seen in the world 'outside' or
in the mind's world 'inside', no longer is a show of that world
only, an epiphany, but is a seed, a generative point of the
inner and outer."

Robert Duncan, "The H. D. Book," TriQuarterly, 1968

"In this tele-topological mode, as the *punctum* regains its
primary importance as light and suddenly becomes prime
matter, transparence becomes a substance, a new material
which is not exactly space/time and which is not properly
analyzed, or filed, until one has attained a degree of
unsuspected purity."

Paul Virilio, *The Lost Dimension*

DZ: **Pratibha***

> After the ball is over, after the Krell
> leave the machine enabling themselves
> to return their true heritage, my crystal set
> picks up Your Hit Parade, original
> live broadcasts I have to shush
> even the air to hear, even the blood
> to my brain, that seashell. Though I have
> no answer, can't finish life's sentences
> yet, can't grasp the equal as opposite,
> the bow still threads this feathered shaft
> through bright axe-heads to restore
> the boss' daughter, who must've known
> all along she'd go home with the one
> who brought her, humming their song

> * "Because the whole sentence meaning is
> inherently present in the mind of each person,
> it is quite possible for the *pratibha* of the *sphota*
> to be grasped by the listener even before the
> whole sentence has been uttered."

> Harold G. Coward, *The Sphota Theory of Language*

IV: Jammin' out of The Jam

At the "Soul in Buffalo" conference in Buffalo (November 18-20, 2010) celebrating *a curriculum of the soul*, Charles Palau, sommelier and Clarke's frequent musical companion, when asked what he had done in the '70s and '80s, replied: "Jack Clarke's homework." He had good company:

> Gerrit Lansing belongs to that much-maligned group "the Olson cult," "the last all-male group in the U.S. gathered around a particular poet" (Marjorie Perloff). They are, perhaps, the most impressive array of unread writers this century. Taking John Clarke's Institute of Further Studies as their measure, I count the following among their members: John Clarke, Albert Glover, David Tirrell, Robert Duncan, Michael McClure, Michael Bylebyl, Anselm Hollo, John Wieners, Robin Blaser, Joanne Kyger, Ed Sanders, Alice Notley, Robert Grenier, George Butterick, James Koller, Duncan McNaughton, Daniel Zimmerman, Edgar Billowitz, and George Butterick. (Friedlander)

"All-male" aside, Jack Clarke and Al Glover inspired the dedication that has kept this unprecedented project compelling for over 40 years. Jack invited me into that company in 1972, assigning me the fascicle on Perspective—'homework' to which I devoted much of the next two years. I lit a candle in the sunshine of my gratitude for that sort of inspiring trust in a letter to Gale H. Carrithers, Jr., then Chair of the English Department at SUNY Buffalo, supporting Jack's promotion to full professor:

> . . . I met Professor Clarke fifteen years ago, when I enrolled in his Blake course. For the first time, it was obvious that something new was going on. It took me about three weeks to adjust to the novelty of his approach and to appreciate its singularity.
>
> . . . A central value [of his approach] is 'watchfulness.' One is not allowed easily to assume that a meaningful point of view can be taken 'from the outside,' or through some critical apparat, but is invited to hazard that one is at every moment immersed in a mythical world and responsive to its dynamic. By accepting its ubiquity as a working hypothesis one is given, like Archimedes, a place to stand from which to move the world. But unlike Archimedes', whose place is ideal, the standpoint of 'causal mythology' is in the world—so much so that the natural man is continually tempted to forget its immanence. It is this forgetfulness Professor Clarke corrects, by presenting information either as furthering the overall investigation of a subject or as specifying the nature of an individual, concrete relationship. (Letter 27 March 1978)

The eroticized language endemic in contemporary mainstream writing and speech, shackled to the moment, "ruining life in pursuit of / itself rather than the ongoing struggle with error" (*EoTS* 14) gives way in *The End of This Side* (1979) to a Blakean situation of States. Jack does not attempt to recreate the experience of moments valorized by memory. A scientist of the imagination—not a necromancer—"by allowing rune to defeat image" he turns from the atomism of an accretion of images as a vehicle for truth to a specification of the fields of truth of events: a process which involves the naming of states, virtual and manifest—his "transverse alternate to image-subjugation" (*EoTS* 26). "It's not what people are saying," he once explained. "It's the feeling gluing it together as a *word*." And in an epigraph to "A Poet's Job Is to Act OUT," he quotes Emerson: "We need not much mind what people please to say, but what they must say" (*In the Analogy* 144). He makes this especially clear in "Awake to Yourself," where he says that the "form of epic writing" which poetry must engage

... is no mimetic multiple of temporal
usurpation, that it is the same as Homer's creative
thrust, which is the same for every Romantic lover who
lived past forty to protect his children from natural
bodies of off-the-wall information that won't hold up. (*EoTS* 5)

In Twitter-land, where nearly all information has reached a level of confessional banality immune to thought, Jack's exhortation to the poets rings even more urgently prophetic. As Mike Boughn said in his eulogy, quoting Jack's comment that at the beginning of Blake's *Job* their musical instruments hang in trees, but at the end the family holds them, "The point is not to be perfect. The point is to play."

V: Sheet Music

June 19, 1986

Daniel John Zimmerman
44 New York Avenue
Metuchen, New Jersey
08840

Dear Dan,
    Since I speak only Venusian and am still
just learning to write Sirian, and have no Martian
at all—I am sending the enclosed letter along to
you. If you are able to respond, please extend my
regrets and high regard. I realize your own con-
siderable Tellurian demands have kept you of late
from completing your Martian studies, but I believe
you have enough Equites to get through. Please don't
be put off by the presumed difference in location,
which is only an editorial convention to humor the
ontic disposition of an estranged readership.

                              Fraternally yours,
                              JACK

    cc: David Levi Strauss

—and once when, particularly hard up, I asked to borrow $10 Jack wrote me the following "check." (I would have spent the ten.)

DZ: on, you huskies

when he got through smiling
nothing was left to say.

he broke the sonic barrier
in a jet-propulsion plane.

it was a Buick.
no one knew what to expect.

go ahead I'll be your Spectre
Jack said standing behind me.

the first thing to be overcome,
the memory of the Golden Age.

(*Perspective*)

[1] Quotations from **BLAKE/EPISTEMOLOGY: STANCE I:**

Distance

Going forth and returning wearied

The nature of infinity is this: That every thing has its
Own Vortex and when once a traveler thro' Eternity
Has pass'd that Vortex, he perceives it roll backward behind
His path, into a globe itself infolding like a sun,
Or like a moon, or like a universe of starry majesty,
While he keeps onwards in his wondrous journey on the earth,
Or like a human form, a friend with whom he liv'd benevolent.
As the eye of man views both the east & west encompassing
Its vortex, and the north & south with all their starry host,
Also the rising sun & setting moon he views surrounding
His corn-fields and his valleys of five hundred acres square,
Thus is the earth one infinite plane, and not as apparent
To the weak traveler confin'd beneath the moony shade.
Thus is the heaven a vortex pass'd already, and the earth
A vortex not yet pass'd by the traveler thro Eternity.

Substance

What are those golden builders doing?

The great City of Golgonooza: fourfold toward the north,
And toward the south fourfold, & fourfold toward the east & west,
Each within other toward the four points: that toward
Eden, and that toward the World of Generation,
And that toward Beulah, and that toward Ulro.
These are the four Faces towards the Four Worlds of Humanity
In every Man. Ezekiel saw them by Chebar's flood.
And every one has three regions, Childhood, Manhood & Age;
But the gates of the tongue, the western gate, in them is clos'd,
Having a wall builded against it, and thereby the gates
Eastward & Southward & Northward are incircled with flaming fires.

Constance

Oh that Death & Annihilation were the same!

There is a Negation, & there is a Contrary
The Negation must be destroy'd to redeem the Contraries.
The Negation is the Spectre, the Reasoning Power in Man:
This is a false Body, an Incrustation over my Immortal
Spirit, a Selfhood which must be put off & annihilated away.
To cleanse the Face of my Spirit by Self-Examination,
To bathe in the Waters of Life, to wash off the Not Human,
I come in Self-annihilation & the grandeur of Inspiration.
These are the Sexual Garments, the Abomination of Desolation,
Hiding the Human Lineaments as with an Ark & Curtains.
Altho' our Human Power can sustain the severe contentions
Of Friendship, our Sexual cannot, but flies into the Ulro.
Hence arose all our terrors in Eternity; & now remembrance
Returns upon us; are we Contraries, O Milton, Thou & I?
O Immortal, how were we led to War the Wars of Death?

Instance

Labour well the Minute Particulars, attend to the Little ones

Let the Human Organs be kept in their perfect Integrity.
At will Contracting into Worms or Expanding into Gods
And then, behold! what are these Ulro Visions of Chastity?
Then as the moss upon the tree, or dust upon the plow,
Or as the sweat upon the labouring shoulder, or as the chaff
Of the wheat floor, or as the dregs of the sweet wine-press:
 Such are these Ulro Visions; for tho' we sit down within
The plowed furrow, list'ning to the weeping clods till we
Contract or Expand Space at will, or if we raise ourselves
Upon the chariots of the morning, Contracting or Expanding Time,
Every one knows we are One Family, One Man blessed for ever.

Works Cited

Boughn, Mike. "A Memorial Statement by Mike Boughn for John Clarke, read July 23, 1992, at the First Presbyterian Church." *ArtVoice,* July 1992.

Campbell, Joseph. *The Mythic Image.* Bollingen Series C. Princeton: Princeton UP, 1974.

Clarke, John. "BLAKE / EPISTEMOLOGY: STANCE I." *Anonym 4.* Ed. Mark Robison and Daniel Zimmerman. Buffalo, 1969.

_____. *From Feathers to Iron: A Concourse of World Poetics.* San Francisco: Tombouctou/Convivio, 1987.

_____. *In the Analogy.* Toronto/Buffalo: shuffaloff, 1997.

_____. Letter to Daniel Zimmerman. 16 December 1982.

_____. "Check" to Daniel Zimmerman. n.d. (c. 1972)

_____. *The End of This Side.* Bowling Green, OH: Black Book, 1979.

_____. "The Opening of the Western Gate Upanishad." *The Western Gate.* Buffalo: 1970.

_____. Daniel Zimmerman. *blue horitals.* Amman, Jordan: Oasii, 1997.

Friedlander, Ben. Review of Gerrit Lansing, *Heavenly Tree Soluble Forest.* http://wings.buffalo.edu/epc/ezines/spt/signals2.html.

Keynes, Geoffrey, ed. *The Complete Writings of William Blake* with all the Variant Readings. London: The Nonesuch Press / New York: Random House, 1957.

Layard, John. "The Malekulan Journey of the Dead." *Spiritual Disciplines.* Ed. Joseph Campbell. Bollingen XXX (4). New York: Pantheon Books, 1960.

Maud, Ralph. "Charles Olson's archaic postmodernism." *Minutes of the Charles Olson Society* #42 (September 2001). http://www. charlesolson.ca/Files/archaic1.htm

Zimmerman, Daniel. *Post-Avant.* Columbus, OH: Pavement Saw, 2002.

_____. "guide book." Unpublished. 2011.

_____. Letter to Gale H. Carrithers, Jr., 27 March 1978.

_____. *Perspective.* A curriculum of the soul #20. Canton, NY: Institute of Further Studies, 1974.

Born in 1933 in Ohio, John Clarke always insisted he was from Winesburg. A William Blake scholar, he taught at the State University of New York at Buffalo for 29 years. He co-edited of *The Niagara Frontier Review* and *The Magazine of Further Studies*, and edited ***intent. a newsletter of talk, thinking, and document.*** He was Director of The Institute of Further Studies and, with Albert Glover, general editor of *A Curriculum of the Soul.* His books include *From Feathers to Iron: A Concourse of World Poetics* and several books of poetry including *Fathar III, Gloucester Sonnets, The End of This Side,* and *In the Analogy.*

"In teaching I apply the end of 20,000 years. For *poesis* I have had an affinity with Olson's 'the first sound realized in a church forever'; in this instance, the mechanism of analogy gives a chaos-maker an index of his capacity to put up or shut up."

Made in the USA
Columbia, SC
23 July 2017